MERRY CHRISTMAS
MOMENTS

51 Stories About the Wonder of Christmas

MERRY CHRISTMAS MOMENTS

51 Stories About the Wonder of Christmas

COMPILED AND EDITED BY YVONNE LEHMAN

GRACE PUBLISHING

Royalties for this book are donated to Samaritan's Purse.

MERRY CHRISTMAS MOMENTS

51 Stories About the Wonder of Christmas

ISBN-13: 978-1-60495-033-5

From Samaritan's Purse

We so appreciate your donating royalties from the sale of the books *Divine Moments, Christmas Moment, Spoken Moments, Precious Precocious Moments, More Christmas Moments, Stupid Moments, Additional Christmas Moments, Loving Moments,* and now, *Merry Christmas Moments* to Samaritan's Purse.

What a blessing that you would think of us! Thank you for your willingness to bless others and bring glory to God through your literary talents. Grace and peace to you.

Their Mission Statement:

Samaritan's Purse is a nondenominational evangelical Christian organization providing spiritual and physical aid to hurting people around the world.

Since 1970, Samaritan's Purse has helped victims of war, poverty, natural disasters, disease, and famine with the purpose of sharing God' s love through his son, Jesus Christ.

Go and do likewise.
Luke 10:37

You can learn more by visiting their website at
www.samaritanspurse.org.

Dedication

Dedicated to
Terri Kalfas, who saw the beauty
and value of sharing praise in
Divine Moments
Christmas Moments
Spoken Moments
Precious, Precarious Moments
More Christmas Moments
Stupid Moments
Additional Christmas Moments
Why? Titanic Moments
Loving Moments

and

to the 50 authors who shared their stories
for this compilation
without compensation
just for the thrill of being useful
and being part of the mission work of
Samaritan's Purse,
who receives all the royalties
from the sale of these books.

Contents

About the Cover Photo *Gigi Graham* 9

Introduction *Yvonne Lehman* 10

1. BROKE…at Christmastime! *Yvonne Lehman* 11

2. Hold On: A Holiday Lesson in Humility *Tez Brooks* 14

3. A Favorite Gift *Lauren Craft* 17

4. The First Christmas *Rebecca Carpenter* 19

5. A Flame of Love *Charlotte Adelsperger* 21

6. When Bells Ring *Pat Jeanne Davis* 23

7. All Is Bright *Julie Dibble* 26

8. A Hero's Words *Alice Klies* 30

9. Lights, Camera, Action *AimeeAnn Blythe* 35

10. Matilda's Christmas Escape *Betty Mason Arthurs* 37

11. Mary's Son *Lola Di Giulio De Maci* 40

12. Trinity's Grace *Vicki H. Moss* 41

13. Rudolph and I Are Buddies *Peggy Ellis* 49

14. Christmas Star *Dr. Jayce O'Neal* 51

15. A Good Eye *Terri Elders* 53

16. Christmas Blessing in Checkout Lane 12 *Sheryl M. Baker* 56

17. A New Song *Kristin Tobin Dossett* 59

18. A Gift Unwrapped *Cynthia Howerter* 61

19. When Christmas Comes in January *Lola Di Giulio De Maci* 65

20. The Offhand Christmas *Terri Elders* 67

21. Love Notes in the Snow *Annmarie B. Tait* 71

22. The Christmas Wish Books *Gayle Fraser* 74

23. Messengers of Mercy *Lola Di Giulio De Maci* 77

24. Tradition *Alice Klies* 80

25. A Father Who Never Leaves *Karen Friday* 82

26. Is That All? *Tommy Scott Gilmore, III* 85

27. A Lasting Transition...hmm, Tradition *Andrea Merrell* 87

28. A Stroll to Remember *Helen L. Hoover* 89

29. My Red Balloon *Samantha Landy* 91

30. Waiting for the Surprise *Diana Leagh Matthews* 94

31. Our Beautiful Christmas Trees *Beverly Hill McKinney* 96

32. What Did You Get for Christmas? *Tommy Scott Gilmore, III* 98

33. Storefront Ministry *Mary E. McQueen* 102

34. Baloney Salad and Fruitcake *Karen Lynn Nolan* 105

35. I Am Bethlehem *Judith Vander Wege* 109

36. There's a Star in the East *Mary E. McQueen* 111

37. Christmas Azalea *Andrea Merrell* 113

38. It Took a Miracle *Sally Wilson Pereira* 114

39. Unforgettable Christmas Gifts *Colleen L. Reece* 117

40. The Greatest Christmas Present *Robert B. Robeson for Rosemary Luebke* ... 120

41. A Gift for God This Christmas *Deborah M. Presnell* 125

42. Christmas Presence *Diana C. Derringer* 129

43. Five Ways to Bless Your Home During Advent *Dr. Rhett H. Wilson, Sr.* ... 134

44. Where Is Baby Jesus? *Norma C. Mezoe* 137

45. After Christmas *Charlotte Adelsperger* 139

46. A Christmas Prayer *Suzanne Liggitt* 140

47. Where's the Gravy? A Southern Tradition at Christmas *Karen Friday* 144

48. Growing the Gift of Prayer *Lydia E. Harris* 146

49. Christmas...Why Bother? *Toni Armstrong Sample* 148

50. Sharing the Gospel from My Exploding Closet *Beverly Varnado* 151

51. Putting Christmas Away *Norma C. Mezoe* 154

Divine Moments Series Guidelines 155

About the Authors 157

About the Cover Photo

The children enjooying the pictures in the book *One Wintry Night*, that my mother, Ruth Graham, wrote, are her great-grandchildren, my grandchildren. They are now grown and have children of their own and Mother has been in heaven for many years. This beautiful picture reminds me of how fast time passes and how important it is to teach the next generation.

Christmas was celebrated with much anticipation and joy in our home, but Jesus was always the center. After all, it is His birthday.

Sadly, now Christmas has become mostly about decorations and gifts and somehow Jesus has been lost in the wrappings. This is cause for inventory… what are we passing on to our children and grandchildren and yes, even our great-grandchildren? How do we celebrate Christmas and what are we teaching our children about the meaning of this Holy Night?

One Wintry Night…yes, it was a very special night.

The night Jesus was born.

We call it Christmas!

~ Gigi Graham

Introduction

Many thanks to all the authors who have contributed to each of the
Divine Moments series,
and at this time of year, particularly
Christmas Moments,
More Christmas Moments, Additional Christmas Moments,
and to this compilation, *Merry Christmas Moments*

We sincerely hope you enjoy this book.
At the end of the book, you may see how you might contribute
to the Divine Moments series.

HAPPY READING and MERRY CHRISTMAS!

Yvonne Lehman

BROKE...at Christmastime!

1

On December 12, 2016, I became literally broken — physically. Then I discovered the truth in 1 Corinthians 12:12, 26 (NLT): The human body has many parts, but the many parts make up only one body...If one part suffers, all the parts suffer with it....

There I was, 20 minutes before 14 Sunday school class members were to arrive for a Christmas party at my beautifully decorated home, the flocked Christmas tree beside the fireplace, two tables set with lovely china, crystal glasses, cloth napkins, aromas of meat concoctions in the crock pot and oven, candles glowing and emitting their holiday scents. Dirty Santa gifts festively wrapped. My *Let It Snow* novel ready to be given to each. Perfect!

So, in my upstairs bedroom I swung my left leg onto my high bed and tied the laces of my black 4-inch heeled suede ankle bootie. As I was leaning back to bring the shoe off the bed, the covers clutched my bootie, I lost my balance, but the covers of the unmade bed wouldn't turn loose and my leg wouldn't come with the rest of my body.

A fleeting thought of *don't break your hip or back* prompted me in a nanosecond to fall to the side while my bootie is still on the bed. The next thing I know I'm gaping at a weird twisted thing where an arm used to be, a band of swelling flesh replacing a wrist, and limp extremities instead of fingers.

My goodness, that was as freaky as when a writers group critiques a manuscript and you can only sit silent, feeling the horror and pain while your "perfect" creation is becoming something unrecognizable and you know it will never be the same again.

Anyway, the next minutes were filled with contortions, crawling, squirming, elbowing across the room, getting a workout more strenuous than my *30-Day Shred* DVD, wondering how to stand or find the phone while left hand holds an appendage that might drop off or, if it gets fatter, could explode.

Long story short — I finally managed to reach the phone and contact my daughter, Lori, and we got ready for the trip to the hospital while guests were arriving. Lori, our Sunday school teacher, told them to stay and enjoy the party, which they seem delighted to do. After all, everything looked and smelled perfect…except me.

At the ER, the arm was confirmed to be broken (hmmm), and we were sent to the aptly named Waiting Room. The entire process lasted over five hours. Lori took pictures, emailed family, friends, partiers, et. al., giving them an overview of happenings. She's a scriptwriter, and you know, to a writer everything is a story.

> She wrote: "I hate to say this, but it was a wonderful time with my mother, despite the circumstances. She was given great numbing medication. We brainstormed for her next book, *Broken Moments*, and made plans for a New Year Sunday school party in January. I prayed while the doctor and nurse pulled Mom's arm back into place and the doc was impressed with how well she handled the setting of her wrist."

My perception was slightly different. The smiling doctor was coming toward me, holding a weapon that looked like a skewer, or spike, or rod and he was saying, "We'll see about numbing this," and the nurse was telling Lori she had fainted twice while watching the procedure. Lori asked if there was anything she could do. I say, "Pray." She prayed aloud while I watched, and felt the doctor gouge, shove, grimace, saying he's trying to find the crease in which he will dispense pain-killing medication. He took a looooong time and what came to my mind is "sadistic."

I do think the prayer worked — the nurse didn't faint.

Finally, after being pulled apart, wrapped, x-rayed, I am incapacitated inside a cast from above the elbow to below the first knuckles on the five-pronged appendage. It was as useless as that story having been rejected by an editor or critiqued by a writers group.

My broken book is like an arm in a cast — useless. Like the body, if one part is broken, all other parts suffer with it. To be functional, readjustment is necessary.

During the weeks that followed, I had to rely on others at times, was challenged to learn new ways. My writing looked like a child's in first grade. But they learn. With time and effort, I could learn.

After removal of the cast, the doctor said there might be nine months before the arm regained previous strength. Hey, don't we call our books our babies? Think of all the changes that take place, leading to that delivery when many women say, "Never again!" But that's forgotten as they hold the most wonderful miraculous of God's creation in their arms.

Book delivery is something like that. All the "helpful" criticism, changes, lovely words deleted, new ways of presenting the initial idea, the cutting, adding, and the book will never be the same and you feel like Mark Twain who wrote, "If I'd known what a trouble it was to make a book I wouldn't a tackled it and ain't going to no more."

My arm hurts when I force movement, weight bearing, flexibility. But I'm told that if I endure the pressure and pain, in time it can be stronger than ever.

Hmmm, isn't that what was said about that manuscript?

I get my books all gussied up, but after discovering it's weak, going to be incapacitated for awhile, has broken parts, and healing will take time, it hurts. I can't take my creative/craft expertise for granted. I'm just one move away from needing to be worked on, body or book. At any time I might have to say, as did David in Psalm 31:12 KJV, "I am a broken vessel."

During my recuperating time I read a comforting devotion of Charles Stanley's based on Matthew 14:22-34. Stanley commented that we should ask the Lord for his presence in the midst of our trouble. He will provide strength to endure and wisdom as we go through the storm. And, as I said, to a writer, everything is a story.

And…good comes from everything. See, I got an article out of the experience. Oops! Better wait to find out if my readers think it needs… surgery.

At least I learned a lesson last Christmas, to smooth the bed covers before tying my stiletto booties.

~ Yvonne Lehman

2

Hold On: A Holiday Lesson in Humility

Christmas shopping is stressful for me. It seems I'm forever trying to hold on to something while shopping — my coat, my shopping cart, my sanity. Then I have everyone else asking me to hold things.

"Hold my hand, Daddy."

"Hold my purse, Honey."

"Hold these up and see if they fit."

"Hold your horses, Sir. The check-out line starts back there." *That's a lot of holding when I can barely hold my* bladder.

It was after one of these particularly joyous shopping excursions when I forgot to hold one of the most important things — my tongue.

We were on the freeway; my daughters, my wife and I trying to rush home for yet another neighborhood party. If I could get home quickly enough, we might be able to toss some frozen mini-quiches in the oven, slip into those kitschy red sweaters we have and walk down to the Joneses for a painful night of eggnog with dips.

Don't get me wrong, the dips are nice, and the Jones have a beautiful home.

In the car seat, our two-year-old daughter began whimpering something about Santa. I ignored it, trying to pay attention to the immense holiday traffic. In front of us, a fir tree on wheels traveling the break-neck speed of thirty mph, was a reminder of yet another thing to buy before Christmas Eve. The other two lanes were filled with cars zipping past us like hummingbirds in a hurricane. It was unlikely I'd be changing lanes anytime soon.

As I crept along the interstate, I was anxious about decorating the house. Dreading the climb into the attic and pulling down all the boxes — more boxes every year. No matter how diligently I pack, the next Christmas I

14

always find a misplaced candle — or what used to be a candle — in one of the boxes. There's always that sickening moment when I spot it from across the attic. It's that familiar oily, red stain on the outside of the box that screams, "You did it again, idiot!" One year it was in the box with the lights. The wax had hardened around the lights like cheese on a plate of cold nachos.

I shook my head. *Why do I bother each year? I take lights from the inside of the attic, only to hang them on the outside of the attic? Am I insane?*

My daughter's fussing got louder, snapping me back from my thoughts. It was escalating into a cry. I turned on the radio, hoping to drown her out. They were playing the same song I'd heard twenty-five times that week and frankly, I was sick of it. In the midst of all the traffic and a wailing child, it was the last tune I cared to hear.

My child got louder. I bit my lip. *Really kid?*

Suddenly, I figured out what her problem was. Earlier my wife and I noticed the large display in the center of the mall, complete with a candy cane throne for Santa. We hadn't stopped to visit him while shopping. At the time, we gave each other a knowing glance — code for "I'm not spending $100 for photos of my girls sitting in a stranger's lap." So we distracted the kids and avoided the display. Now here we were, almost home free.

"I didn't get to see Santa!" my little darling screamed from the back seat. As always, she insisted on pulling others into her drama.

She's so much like me, and I love her for it.

But today, I'd listened to it long enough. I'd had enough of the traffic, the mobs of shoppers, and the stinking radio. Blood was rushing to my temples like magma. Unable to hold my temper any longer, I allowed the day's activities to carry me cruelly to this Mt. Saint Helens moment. Spinning the radio off, I yelled into the rear-view mirror "That's enough! Santa's dead."

As soon as the words left my mouth, I knew I'd messed up. What could I do? The words were out there, stinging my daughter's heart like a giant bar of soap in the eyes of childlike reverie and imagination.

She began wailing, "No! Santa's not dead, is he?"

My wife looked at me then shook her head. "Smooth."

I sighed, sinking low in the driver's seat of the mini-van. Minimizing is always my first defense. So, to look unconcerned about the blunder, I pretended to check my side mirrors for traffic — anything to appear nonchalant. Inside I was kicking myself. *Can this day get any worse? Maybe no one noticed.*

"There goes that Father-of-the-Year award," my wife said, staring out the passenger side window.

"I know, I know. I'll fix it. Let's just get home first."

When we arrived, I took our little girl aside, hugged her, and apologized for being such a Grinch. Apologizing to a toddler was a good lesson in humility for me. I am far from the perfect dad and this probably wouldn't be the last time I lose it or say something I regret.

That night, I started the splendid habit of saying "I'm sorry" when I blow it with my kids. To this day, it's proven invaluable in sustaining my authenticity as the spiritual leader of our family.

For our two-year old, my apology and admission of wrong was her tree topper for the night. She put her thumb in her mouth and sank into my arms. For the next twenty minutes we sat in her room snuggling while *Silent Night* played from the stereo. We were having a moment.

I had spent the day holding things I didn't want to. Now I was holding something and I never wanted to let go.

Needless to say, we were a bit late for the Jones' party. That's okay, those dips could wait.

- Tez Brooks

3

A Favorite Gift

I admit it. One of my favorite parts of Christmas is tearing through wrapping paper and catching the first glimpse of a new gift. One year, my favorite gift came a few weeks early, and it wasn't in a wrapped box. It arrived on the day a surprise ice storm hit — the same day as our yearly Christmas party for children.

Presents were waiting in the fellowship hall for each boy and girl, and a potluck lunch was planned. Most of all, I looked forward to presenting the real meaning of Christmas. Some of the children attending had a parent in prison. With others, their parents simply couldn't afford presents that year.

Since I was hosting the party, I decided to leave two hours earlier than guests would arrive. At 10 A.M., when I stepped outside the front door, my heart sank. Ice was everywhere — encasing the grass, my car, and the street. Perhaps, I thought, the sunshine would brighten and melt the ice in time for the party.

Father, I can't cancel this event, can I?

Walking slowly to avoid slipping on the ice, I made two trips to the car, carrying bags of supplies. When I sat in my driver's seat and reached into my purse, my nerves started pounding. The keys were missing. I'd left them on the table in the foyer. I'd just locked the doors and my husband was out of town for the morning.

Father, is this another sign we shouldn't have the party? I want the children to hear about you, but I don't want anyone to get hurt in this weather.

Something in my heart willed me to keep fighting. Too much planning had gone into this event. Thirty guests had been invited and at least a dozen volunteers were looking forward to it.

Taking a deep breath, I pulled out my phone. With cold fingers, I dialed my dear friend Kari, who always seems to know what to do. She offered to pick me up, but it would take too long. Because she lives in a wooded area with a long driveway; she was more stuck than I was.

Father, help me get to this party in time.

I dialed more numbers, but didn't reach anyone. Sitting in the car, I pulled my jacket closer to stay warm.

An hour passed and the sun rose in the sky. The ice was melting so quickly that it sounded like a trickling creek. A good sign, but I was still stranded.

Then an incoming call trilled from a number I didn't recognize.

"Lauren, where are you?" The sound of my friend Debbie's voice was like the warmth of a fireplace.

"Debbie, please pick me up. I'm locked out of my house!"

Ten minutes later, Debbie and another friend, Angela, pulled up to my house. Relieved, I hopped inside, supplies in hand.

When I walked into the church fellowship hall, the other volunteers had already decorated the room with red and green tablecloths, balloons, and shiny garland.

I presented the Christmas story to the guests. Afterwards, one of the moms pulled me aside. "I've been trying a long time to get my daughter interested in praying and reading her Bible." Her brown eyes glistened. "She never seemed to listen. After your talk, she told me she wants to let Jesus into her heart."

I wanted to jump up and down. The light in her face told me she wanted to do the same.

I said, "I just trickled a little bit of water on the seed you already planted."

She nodded. "I think it was good to hear from another adult. Someone other than her mommy."

We laughed and hugged. She wiped her eyes.

After the event, my husband was back in town and picked me up. As we walked to his car, I looked at the ground outside. The road wasn't even damp — not a trace of ice anywhere. The only thing that lingered was the memory of a child giving her heart to Jesus and a loving mother, shedding tears of pure joy.

That was the best gift any of us could have received.

~ Lauren Craft

4

The First Christmas

Weary hooves clopped on cobblestones. With each step, the pregnant teenager winced. Stoically, she endured the long, miserable journey and looked forward to a comfortable bed.

Because of Caesar Augustus's decree, which required a census of the entire Roman world, pilgrims roamed the overflowing streets of Bethlehem. Joseph led the donkey down narrow passageways in search of a room. Time after time he heard the same answer, "There is no room."

Mary's pleading eyes begged for a place to rest. In desperation, Joseph accepted the innkeeper's offer of a place in the stable. He helped her down from the donkey but lamented the unsuitable conditions. She gladly lay on the bed of hay. Odors of damp hay and manure mingled, but the exhausted couple hardly noticed.

Mary's eyes opened and she clutched her stomach as pain gripped her. Far from home, her only support was the inexperienced man at her side. But his strong, carpenter hands helped deliver the perfect baby.

She cradled the promised child in swaddling cloths. Tenderly, she placed him in the trough filled with hay. Jesus slept peacefully in the humble stable while the couple marveled at the fulfillment of the angelic prophecy.

Darkness settled over the rocky hills near the village of Bethlehem. Away from the commotion of the crowds, shepherds watched their flocks beneath the twinkling sky.

From the blackness, an angel appeared. The terrified men stared at the spectacle before them.

The angel spoke, "Do not be afraid. I bring you good news of great joy that will be for all the people. Today in the town of David a Savior has been born to you; he is Christ the Lord. This will be a sign to you. You will find a baby wrapped in cloths and lying in a manger." (Luke 2: 10-12 NIV)

Instantly, a blaze of light illuminated the sky. A multitude of angels sang praises. "Glory to God in the highest. Peace on earth. Good will to all men." Darkness returned after the angels disappeared. The bewildered shepherds tried to make sense of what they had seen and heard. Even though the incident seemed impossible, they agreed to go into Bethlehem to search for the baby.

Sandaled feet ran over rocks. Excited men passed stable after stable. Then a tiny cry beckoned them. Joseph stood guard beside his family. Only after he recognized the silent reverence of the shepherds did he step aside for them to enter. At the sight of the baby, each visitor knelt in awe. Before them lay the Savior the angel promised.

With a new confidence and boldness, the simple, uneducated men hurried to share the news of Jesus' birth. Their words amazed the throngs of people in Bethlehem. The shepherds continued praising God for all they had seen and heard.

None of the events that night made sense to those waiting for a king to deliver them. God used uneducated, young, lonely, marginalized characters who listened, obeyed, and shared the good news.

Even now, He often uses those the world sees as unsuccessful, untrained, ordinary, and downtrodden to inspire and tell His story.

~ Rebecca Carpenter

5

A Flame of Love

My childhood Christmases were filled with simple but delightful surprises. I'll never forget the Christmas Eve when I first saw a candle in the birdbath in our backyard. A magical flame flickered from a large red candle covered with a hurricane lantern. My twin sister, Alberta, my little brother, Wally, and I pressed our noses to the frosted window in awe.

Joining in the excitement, our parents quickly explained, "Santa has marked our house. That candle must mean he's coming back tonight when everyone's asleep." We children flew straight to our beds.

Of course, we woke up early on Christmas morning and scampered into the living room. There we saw a fully decorated and lighted tree surrounded by piles of presents. The scent of fresh pine filled the room.

"Look at the tree — and toys!" Alberta said as Wally inched closer. For a glorious moment I stared at the wonderful sight, my heart pounding. The air around me seemed to crackle with excitement.

Later on Christmas Day, our father gently took each of us to the kitchen window. "See, the candle is still burning out there," he proclaimed. A wave of joy rippled through me, and I felt our home was marked in a special way.

A few years later we learned that our father, so creative and loving, had slipped outside and placed the candle while Mother kept us distracted. For us, it came to symbolize our family's closeness and a sense of Christ's light in the world, and each year, the candle continued to appear on Christmas Eve.

For many years after our parents, Walter and Mary Rist, first surprised us, the tradition has lived on in our adult lives. Each year on December 24 my brother Wally secretly lit a candle in a birdbath for his children.

When Mother became a widow, Alberta and her husband made sure that our childhood home had a lighted candle in the birdbath. One Christmas Eve when Mother was ninety, she sat in her wheelchair and gazed toward that light with dim and misty eyes. Later she said, "I saw it out there, but I could feel it in my heart."

Now our grown children and their families gather at our house on Christmas Eve. While carols play on the stereo, we rip open packages with joy and laughter. Later that night we bring out a supper, and bow our heads for a prayer of thanks. But whenever we go to the kitchen window, we can see a flickering beacon — a glowing red candle in a lantern.

After midnight, when everyone is gone, my husband Bob and I turn off the lights except for those on the tree. We hold hands. In the stillness, we watch the flame burning outside. It has become a time of nostalgia and deep thanksgiving to God. Special love still marks our home.

- Charlotte Adelsperger

6
When Bells Ring

"It's beginning to look a lot like Christmas."

The words coming from the fellowship hall's sound system rang in Melanie's ear.

She walked toward her spot through a crowded room, rolling a big suitcase filled with books. Today was the church's annual Christmas bazaar and Melanie had been invited to sign her new book and stories published in several anthologies.

She was excited, but there was no carol ringing within her heart. She hoped no one would ask how a thirty-year-old single woman, with no prospects, could be merry and bright.

She heaved a sigh, feeling like the last person who should be writing inspirational stories titled, *All in Good Time* or *Wait and See*.

The woman at the entry had said someone would help her with the table, but she could probably manage. But as she struggled to unfold it, her hand caught a sharp edge, and the table crashed to the floor. An icy knot grew in her stomach as blood pulsed to the surface of her finger.

Great. Blood-smeared books are just what people want for Christmas. She pulled a tissue from her bag and wrapped it around her finger.

"Let me help with that."

She turned and saw a handsome, deep-voiced, blue-eyed, smiling man. He grabbed the table and placed it against a wall decorated with a colorful wreath. "Will that do?"

"Perfect. Thank you."

He motioned toward a corridor. "The restroom is at the end of the hall. There are Band-Aids and peroxide in the cabinet."

"Thanks." she said, and followed his instructions.

When she returned, he was still at her table. He extended his hand. "I'm Jake." He gestured to the large poster with her name in bold lettering. "And you must be Melanie."

She shook his hand, then observed the eye-catching display he'd made with her books. "I didn't expect you to do all this."

"No problem." Jake smiled. "The least I can do for someone donating her proceeds to Northern Home's Christmas fund. Did I get that right?"

Melanie wondered who had told him that. She had been invited here, but it wasn't her home church. Maybe he read it in the paper. She nodded. "The money helps buy gifts for those who otherwise wouldn't receive gifts over the holiday."

"Commendable." He took a step closer to talk over the noise of vendors setting up tables around them and the music that still blared. "I do a little writing myself."

Oh, so that's why he seemed interested. "Always nice to meet a fellow —" Before she could finish her sentence, a woman rushed up to Jake.

"Wonderful to see you this morning, Pastor."

Pastor?

"Good morning, Phyllis. Would you be interested in buying one of these books to raise money for a worthy cause?" He flashed a big smile.

Grateful for Jake's lead-in, Melanie added, "The sale of these make Christmas a little brighter for a poor child."

"Let me see what you've got." Phyllis scanned the titles, then picked up a copy of *Christmas Miracles*. "I'll take this one."

Melanie autographed the book, and Phyllis hastened to another table.

Okay, so he had two reasons for paying her this attention. "So," she said. "You're the pastor of this church…and a writer?"

He grimaced, but his eyes looked playful. "I guess you don't read Jake's weekly column in the local newspaper."

She quickly closed her mouth that had inadvertently opened. "Oh, you're *that* Jake."

Jake rubbed the back of his neck and gave a low chuckle. "Since I'm single, I give advice to singles."

Before she could respond to say she read it faithfully, he was called away.

Over the next hour, several shoppers stopped by Melanie's book table. She answered questions and made a few sales, but kept looking around, wondering what had happened to Jake.

When the crowds thinned out, he returned with a cup of coffee for her. She picked up one of her books. "I'd like to give you this as a thank-you for coming to my rescue." She handed him *Inspiration for Singles*.

"My pleasure," he said warmly. "Would you sign it for me?"

Her pen paused for a moment. Should she write, "To Pastor Jake"? No, he introduced himself as Jake. She signed, "To Jake. Meeting you was a pleasure."

He read the inscription. "Thank you," he said. "This could be useful for my singles' group. We meet here Monday nights at seven. It would be…my pleasure…if you would join us."

No, she mustn't say, "my pleasure," again, so she said, "I would like that."

His deep blue eyes fixed on hers, just long enough to cause that warm feeling to reach her cheeks.

"And I hope you'll read my column next week in *The Review*." He winked. "I think it's going to be "Never Underestimate the Unexpected."

How different the music sounded to Melanie than when she'd entered this room earlier. Outside, Christmas bells were ringing. Somehow, they seemed to be ringing within her heart.

~ *Pat Jeanne Davis*

7
All Is Bright

I was a small girl with a heavy weight on my shoulders. I clipped coupons to prepare for doing my mom's grocery shopping. Her stack of unpaid bills continued to rise. My seventh-grade self could not tolerate her neglect to use this "free money" found in the Sunday paper.

All our family's problems stemmed from lack of money, at least that's how I saw it as a child. Mom's bartending job kept her away from home most nights. I cooked, cleaned, did my homework and tucked in my six-year old brother. Nighttime was fitful. I waited for her key to rattle and the door to burst open.

But sometimes there would be fighting. I'm thankful my brother slept. He wouldn't understand, though honestly neither did I. Peace was a high-priced commodity in our home. We did not have enough money to "get" peace, or joy, or any of the other sentiments expressed in the Christmas carols that played on the radio.

However, my brother and I sang the songs printed in a kids' carol book with pink cover and worn pages.

Silent night
Holy night
All is calm, all is bright
Round yon Virgin, Mother and Child
Holy infant so tender and mild
Sleep in heavenly peace
Sleep in heavenly peace

The aroma of evergreen filled the room while we sang by the tree. My mom shared her love for Christmas with us. Anticipation's pitter-patter sent us out of bed early on Christmas morning in hopes of catching Santa doing his jolly job.

We never prayed or read the Bible or honored Jesus on Christmas, or at all. But "Silent Night" calmed my jumpy insides. The words were beautiful yet so unreachable. Maybe it was the alluring tempo of the song, quite opposite of Mom's yelling nature. For as much tension as there was in our home, I knew Mom loved us. She told us so when she was home and tucked us into bed. But growing up without God's wisdom, holding onto truth was like holding onto a slippy, flippy rainbow trout.

I went through life feeling as though an invisible wall stood between me and peace. Depression overlaid with grief was the foundation of my emotional being. Anger simmered for years after Mom lost her life to cancer. She was forty when she died on December 20th. I was twenty-one. Her death triggered a loneliness deep inside my soul. To me, death was a final sentence to the dirt and worms. I knew nothing of eternal life. I did not know any of us had a Savior.

Christmas became bittersweet. I would feel closest to Mom at that time of year, yet also feel the emptiest. Seeking peace and hope was not a conscious process that I recall. It was like the loneliness was animated with a life of its own. Moaning and droning through the days, my sad heart seemed to suffer. A longing so vast begged me to do something, to find someone, to be happy once and for all.

My soul celebrated marriage as "the one and only answer" to my pent-up, broken emotional life. These expectations set me up for disillusionment. Without God, marriage was not a soul-filler. We loved each other but were not guided by the One who teaches respect and selfless serving.

After Dad died December 15th the year I was thirty-five, my soul gave in to bitterness. My lifelong loneliness came alive again, tugging at my heart. If nobody loved me, I would not have expectations, and I wouldn't get hurt. I might as well hole up here, for I am an orphan.

Except…the God I did not know blessed my marriage with two baby boys, twenty-two months apart. Yes, there was some joy that would temporarily shine in the dark…until the world offered another reason for my spirits to tank.

As an atheist for many years, I questioned every aspect of life that was unfair and unexpected. It seemed every bad thing that could possibly happen, happened to me.

On a whim, the year I turned forty, I went alone to a Christmas Eve service. A woman in my neighborhood had been walking with me, and this was her church. Without knowing where the impulse was coming from, I told my husband I needed to go.

I sat in one of the last pews. Fresh tears filled with old grief streamed over my shame-filled cheeks while trying to sing "Joy to the World." The lights dimmed. Someone handed me a candle holder. The pastor explained how to tip your candle to your neighbor to share the light. I wondered how the darn thing would stay lit with all my blubbering.

When all the flames were aglow, the words to "Silent Night" came on the screen. The voices of togetherness spoke to my lonely heart. Though I could not comprehend it, my ears began to hear something beyond the favorite holiday tune.

This Christmas Eve marked the first time I ever felt the power of God's presence. I did not know Him or His son, but my spirit was calm and sensed some brightness. God was pressing past the stone walls guarding my soul to awaken His child. A sense of safety enveloped me that night in the church. My soul-starved unconscious thought: *Just maybe peace lives here.*

Silent Night ,holy night
Shepherds quake at the sight
Glories stream from heaven afar
Heavenly hosts sing Alleluia
Christ the Savior is born
Christ the Savior is born.

Only God has the power to move people's hearts toward Him. Only Jesus can save people from themselves. Only His supernatural healing power shines light into thick darkness that served evil for generations.

Silent Night, holy night
Son of God, Love's pure light
Radiant beams from Thy holy face
With the dawn of redeeming grace
Jesus. Lord at Thy birth.
Jesus, Lord at Thy birth.

Never underestimate Our Mighty Sovereign God who sacrificed His *Jesus Lord at Thy birth* to redeem His beloved sheep.

It is a humbling experience to write such a story as I bow to Our Holy Source of Light and Life.

Read Psalm 107:2 NLT: Has the Lord redeemed you? Then speak out! Tell others He has redeemed you from your enemies.

~ Julie Dibble

8

A Hero's Words

I stood in the center of the living room. I scanned the entire area. "Where will I put the Christmas tree," I mumbled under my breath? "Where's my so-called Christmas spirit? Gone." I sighed. Still talking out loud I said, "I can't believe I'm even thinking about decorating. For what reason? After all it's just me, two kids and the dog."

I bent over the small boxed artificial Christmas tree, cut the strips of tape that held it together and burst into tears. "This is so stupid," My vocal cords burned from the outburst. I brought my foot back and kicked the box with fury. It slid across the tile floor. My pain this Christmas stemmed from the ugly divorce I'd gone through only months before.

My youngest child, barely eight months old, never understood my tears, but my three-year-old son often asked, "Mommy, why are you crying?" I always made up some silly story that seemed to satisfy him. I was particularly glad I'd left my children with their grandparents for an overnight visit this Christmas Eve. More memories flickered before me like an old fashioned movie.

Had it really been only eight months ago that my husband of five years — on the ride home from the hospital after I'd delivered our daughter — said words I never expected to hear? As I sat in the back seat holding our newborn daughter he said, "I know this is bad timing, but I don't want to be married. I don't think I'm cut out to be a father either."

I felt like someone had punched me in the gut. Bile rose from the bottom of my stomach threatening to move past the back of my teeth.

I can still see the image of my newborn daughter as I pulled her close to my face and stammered, "You're kidding?"

In almost a whisper my husband simply said, "No, I'm not."

I recoiled deep into my seat, silent the rest of the way home.

The thought of my stepmother and dad who waited at home with our son brought more tears that trickled down my cheeks.

When we arrived home, I left the car door open and ran into the house. I gave my daughter to my stepmother and rushed past her toward the bedroom. I closed the door, leaned back against it and sobbed. Seconds later I collapsed to the floor in the bathroom on my knees, with my head over the toilet.

After a long time, I rose and washed my face, swished water in my mouth and gazed at my puffy eyes in the mirror. Then, a soft knock sounded at the door.

"Honey, it's me, Daddy. We know what happened. Let me in. We'll get through this."

I opening the door and fell into Daddy's arms, sobbing against his chest. "Oh Daddy, what will I do?" He had always been my hero, my best friend.

"I don't know sweetheart, but I do know we can handle this as a family. I don't understand at all, but we will be here for you. Right now, you need to pull yourself together for the sake of your children. Dry your eyes. We will go out together. You are a strong woman. You can do this."

The days that followed seemed a blur, until spending Christmas alone with the children settled into my consciousness. The memories that churned their way back into my heart make me angry. "Merry Christmas! Bah humbug!" I screamed. Another kick at the box that held the tree sent it skimming across the floor into a wall. I crumbled into a heap on the floor.

Someone knocked at the door. Who could that be? I couldn't let anyone see me like this. I hollered, "Just a minute." Then, I ran to a mirror on the wall by the front door, dabbed a tissue at my eyes and blew my nose. I hollered again. "I'm coming."

I composed myself by the time I approached the door, but when I opened it, the tears flowed again. Daddy stood in the doorway with a silly reindeer hat cocked sideways on his head and arms full with wrapped packages. "Oh Daddy, what have you done?" Once again my hero stood in front of me just when I needed him.

Daddy pulled a shiny red wagon behind him. The wagon, brimmed full to the edges, held lights, ornaments and packages that made my heart thump with hope. He pointed to his pickup truck parked in front of the house. A huge, fresh cut Christmas tree lay tied in the bed of the truck. My bright-eyed son, bundled in a brand new red coat, sat next to the tree. "Mommy,

Mommy, look what grandpa and I cut down." He stood and clapped his mitten-covered hands together.

My stepmother climbed down from the cab of the truck. She held my daughter who was bundled snug in a sassy blue sweater adorned with snowflakes. "Hey sweetheart. We thought you might need to be cheered up." She embraced me and planted a kiss on the top of my head.

Dad pulled the tree free of its bindings and he and his grandson dragged it through the front door. My stepmother and daughter followed. Together the four of them started to decorate as I watched. I put my hand to my heart and bowed my head. My son giggled as he ran from wagon to tree with each ornament while my daughter played in the tinsel.

I turned and walked to the kitchen. "Hey guys, I'm going to make a pot of hot chocolate. You all look like you need to warm up." A tingle spread through me. I felt my lips curl up at the corners pushing the grimace from my face.

Dad came up behind me. "We'll get through this together," he said. There it was again, Dad's soothing voice.

"Daddy, you always know just what to say. I can't believe you went to all this trouble. Thank you. I love you so much."

"And I love you too." He grabbed my hand and pulled it to his lips and planted a kiss.

"Mommy, Mommy, let's light the tree. It's all done. Santa is going to love it." My son slammed into my knees and wrapped his tiny arms as tight as he could around them.

"Yes, sweetheart, Santa will love it." I followed him to the tree, picked up my daughter and buried my face into the soft folds of her neck. *Yes*, I thought, *we will make this a very merry Christmas.*

The lights from the tree sparkled and made silhouettes that danced on the ceiling. Once again, Dad put his arm around me. "You know, honey, life hands us a bunch of disappointments." He squeezed my shoulder. "But it's up to us to make the choice as to how we are going to react to them. What's your choice going to be?"

I looked deep into his eyes. "Daddy, once again, you've hit the nail on the head. There is absolutely no reason for me to be so sad. I have a wonderful family and I have some really good friends." Just then, the dog rubbed against my leg. "And I even have a loyal dog." I laughed. "Thank you for always coming to my rescue. I am going to choose laughter and joy. I owe this to my children, you and myself."

I put my daughter down next to the tree, turned on my heels, headed toward the kitchen and shouted. "Who wants pizza?"

More giggles sounded from the children. I reached for my cell phone and dialed the nearest pizza store. "Could I please order two large pepperoni pizzas? And by the way, Merry Christmas." I tucked the phone into my jean pocket and turned to Daddy.

"You know, for such a long time, I have been miserable. I've been convinced that I did something wrong to have this happen, you know, the divorce and all. Then, you come along and remind me that it is really my choice to be happy or miserable."

He reached past me to stir the hot chocolate still brewing on the stove. "I know I make it out to be such a black and white decision, but at the same time, I also know that it isn't easy. You are the only one who can decide to let go of the past and make way for whatever the future holds."

"Can I ever forgive him, Daddy? How is this possible? When I found out he had an affair, I thought my heart could never mend. How do I forgive such a thing? I'm still so angry."

"Honey, God reminds us through Scripture that unless we can forgive our trespassers, that He then, cannot forgive our trespasses."

"I know, Daddy. I can say that out loud, but I wonder if my heart really feels it. How do I know I genuinely mean it?"

"I'm not sure of all the answers, sweetheart, but I believe a peace will overcome you and you will just know."

My son bolted through the kitchen door. "Mommy, the pizza's here! Should I get the paper plates?" He skipped to the cupboard.

"Yes, yes baby, get the blue and white ones. Oh, and get the napkins too."

"Okay. Can we eat in the living room by the tree?"

"You bet. Grandpa and I will be right behind you."

My son ran toward the living room with paper plates and napkins tucked under his little arms. "Come on, let's eat."

I smiled at Daddy while tears pooled in my eyes. "Daddy, I have just decided to forgive the past, and step out in faith. Thank you for always being in my corner, for being my hero. I love you."

I wound my hand in a tight grip around Daddy's forearm. Together we walked to the living room. Dad paid for the pizza and then we all gathered on the floor in front of the Christmas tree. Yellow cheese from the pizza dripped from the chins of the children. My son chatted in excited gibberish about the toys Santa would bring.

The doorbell rang again. Who could that be? I swallowed the last bite of my pizza and opened the door. The children's father stood in the doorway with his hands stuffed in his pockets.

"Hi, sorry I didn't call first. Just thought I'd bring the kids their gifts tonight so you could put them under the tree for Christmas morning." He shrugged, looked down at his feet, and then looked up at me.

I took in a deep breath. As I blew it out, the only thing I heard in my mind was the word "choice." Right then, I felt an overwhelming need to say, "Yes, come in." Instead, I leaned close to his head and whispered. "I want you to know, I forgive you."

"What?" He turned pale and started to speak but my son rushed to the door. He screamed, "Daddy, Daddy!" My ex stepped into the living room where my dad and stepmother greeted him with a hug. My son danced around him while his sister waved.

"Daddy, come see the tree that we cut." My son pulled his dad toward the tree.

I looked at Daddy and nodded. He nodded back, raised his hand to his brow in a salute and smiled.

"It feels good," I said. "You are so right. It truly is all about choice. I'm letting go. I'm forgiving him. And God has given me the peace I feel right now."

I did feel good and could wish everyone, "Merry Christmas."

- Alice Klies

9

Lights, Camera, Action

Decorating for Christmas has always been a highlight of the year for me. When I was young and still living in my parents' house, I pleaded to get the decorations out as soon as Thanksgiving dinner was over. Every time a Christmas box was pulled down from the attic, my eyes lit up. There's just something about Christmas — especially the lights — that brightened my spirits on the gloomy days of winter when darkness comes early.

Years later, my sweet, eleven-year-old son, Colton, knew how much I liked decorating for Christmas. One year, we got all the Christmas boxes out with the intention of putting up the lights and decorations a little at a time each night after I came home from work. But Colton wanted to surprise me, so he did it himself. He couldn't wait to show me how he carefully wound the white lights around each baluster and each railing on the deck of our second floor apartment. He was so proud of himself! I gave him a big hug and told him how much help he was to me.

After dinner, we decided to go out on the deck and enjoy his special holiday decoration surprise. He wanted me to sit on the chair while he plugged in the deck lights. When he did, they were so bright I thought I was on a television stage. He had not strung one set of lights. He had strung four. Not wanting to hurt his feelings, I couldn't bring myself to tell him I thought there might be too many lights.

I continued to give him kudos about what a good job he had done. We sat outside basking in the overwhelming glow of all those white lights. When we decided to head inside for the night, he begged me to leave the lights on.

A couple nights later a knock sounded on the door. I looked through the peephole and there stood the apartment maintenance man. He politely told me that the people on the deck next to ours were complaining about the lights. This was not because they were Scrooges, according to the maintenance man, but rather because our lights were so bright that they were keeping the couple awake at night even with their blinds closed.

After he left, I drove around to the loading dock of the Home Depot behind our apartment complex to check out our lights from that distance. There happened to be workers unloading a truck at the time. I pulled up, got out of the car and looked back toward our apartment. I mentioned to the workers that the enormous glow in the distance was from my apartment and they told me they had wondered what was going on over there. There were other Christmas lights in our complex but none as bright as ours. They joked that there was maybe a Hollywood movie crew shooting a sequel to *Christmas Vacation*.

I spent the short drive back deciding how to explain to my son that we would have to remove some of the lights. Not wanting him to feel bad, I gently explained that we did not want to outshine our neighbors. That evening, we took photos of what a magnificent job he had done decorating the deck for Christmas, after which I helped him remove several strands of lights.

Last year Colton sent me a photo of how he had decorated the sidewalk up to the apartment he now shares with his wife. He had penguin and candy cane lights along the walkway, five inflatables on the small grassy area, a wreath on the door and miniature white lights framing his doorway. I guess he never really forgot how good it feels to decorate for the holidays. And even though it's been twenty-three years since my genuinely sweet son went overboard in creating his Christmas surprise for me, I'll never forget the year that he put us on center stage in the Hollywood Lights.

None of the neighbors could outshine us. What a happy holiday!

~ AimeeAnn Blythe

Matilda's Christmas Escape

All winter an icy wind blew over the Niagara Gorge and into our nursing home not far from Niagara Falls, in Lewiston, New York. In the 1970s I worked part-time. As an RN and evening supervisor, my shift was from 3-11 P.M. while my husband cared for our toddler daughter and baby son.

Anne, a nurse's aide, rushed toward me when I arrived at the nursing home. "Mrs. Arthurs," she said breathlessly. "Matilda escaped during lunch."

Before questions could form in my mind, Anne continued. "She walked out wearing only her cotton dress and a thin sweater."

I pulled my heavy coat closer. "The authorities…?"

"Oh, we got her back," Anne said as my thoughts were going in all directions. How could she simply walk out the door on this cold December afternoon? We had newly-installed cameras and buzzing alarms at each door.

I took a deep breath. "How did we get her back?" However, I was thinking, *is this the beginning of a wild Christmas season at Fairland Nursing Home? Will we be losing more confused patients as they search for their old homes and for the sons and daughters who no longer come for visits?*

Anne smiled. "A man who lives in the apartments ten blocks away found Matilda and brought her back. He said she reminded him of his grandmother."

"I'm so glad she's okay. I'm going to her room and check on her. Thanks, Anne."

The aides had already tucked Matilda into bed for a nap. I was grateful she had a normal blood pressure and seemed unhurt. She asked, "Is Sharon coming today?" How should I answer her when we all knew her daughter had died years ago?

Matilda was one of our favorite patients. In her 80s, she entertained us as she chattered nonstop about anything and nothing. In good physical shape, she prowled the halls all day, content to hug and greet strangers and the staff.

We were her beloved family.

I thought of others in this family. It included Patrick, our Irish gentleman, who also roamed the halls and would sing about Ireland and even dance a wobbly jig. He was a large man, "smoked" a pipe and brightened our days as he told us tales of his childhood. We loved him too.

Nellie had suffered numerous strokes and each day we gently restrained her in a wheelchair for her safety and to keep her posture upright. She tried so hard to talk and we pretended to understand her. We parked her near the nurse's station so she wouldn't be alone.

Although her mind was bright and alert, Bess was one of our frail, bedridden patients. Each Sunday her grandson would gently pick her up in his arms, carry her out to his car and treat her to a ride around town.

Each of our patients had interesting backgrounds and stories to tell. But the holidays were difficult. We worried that their families would not visit or bring them gifts or send a card.

Jim, a young father, we later learned, had found Matilda and taken her home to his small apartment, fixed hot tea for her, enjoyed her chatter and loved seeing her with his wife and two small children. He told us, "She reminded me of my grandma. I had to help her." Eventually he found out where she belonged and brought her back. After that, he adopted Matilda, calling her "Grandma" and came often to visit.

In spite of all our efforts to keep the Christmas cheer going, it was a difficult season for most of our patients. But this Christmas Eve, thanks to Matilda's crazy escape, our nursing home buzzed with excitement.

Jim, dressed in a Santa Claus suit, his wife as Mrs. Claus, and their two children as elves, had special gifts for each resident. Undeterred by their limited income, Jim and his family had purchased sweet smelling talcum powder for each of our ladies and Old Spice aftershave for our gentlemen.

Shouting, "Ho, ho, ho, Merry Christmas!" Jim and his family paraded into each room, pulling wrapped packages out of his red cloth bag. They lovingly placed their gifts into the withered hands of each woman and man.

Patients called back, "Merry Christmas!" Some said, "Thank you. God bless you!" They visited Matilda last and watched as she unwrapped her gift.

Despite her confusion, she hugged Jim and his family. "Thank you, Merry Christmas," she said.

Like the wise men who followed a star to Bethlehem, Jim and his young family followed their hearts and with love and compassion gave gifts to the lonely folk who are often forgotten in a nursing home. I imagine Jim's children never forgot the lesson they learned about the true meaning of Christmas.

It's in giving to others that we experience the birth of the Christ child. It's a meaningful lesson I've never forgotten, thanks to Matilda's escape…and Santa Claus Jim.

- Betty Mason Arthurs

Mary's Son

"I love you, my son," Mary whispered softly, as she cradled her newborn son in her arms. "I love you more than all the stars in the sky and all the wildflowers on the mountainside."

The cold night wind crept into the silent corners of the stable, leaving shadows of unwritten messages on splintered walls.
Mary shuddered.
"I wonder where life will take you, my child," she murmured, holding him a little tighter.

Suddenly Mary felt the rush of a violent wind.
She saw her son as a grown man lying in her arms, and she was crying.

"Be careful, my son," she whispered.

Mary picked up her tiny baby and held him close to her heart.
She looked up through an open slat in the stable's roof and saw a million stars,
one glowing with the brilliance of a morning sun.
And she was filled with hope.

"Take care of him, Heavenly Father," she prayed.
"He's just a little boy."

- Lola Di Giulio De Maci

Trinity's Grace

A week before Christmas, in my daughter's kitchen I held a cup of coffee while pondering the meaning of strange happenings. When she came in, I greeted her with, "This morning, I was looking out of the upstairs bedroom window and I saw an angel on your front lawn."

Peyton's eyes widened. "No. Mom, you didn't." When she realized I wasn't kidding, she dared to say, "Where?"

Concerned about what the sighting might mean — and not realizing how my revelation had come across, I said, "Yes. I did. Smack dab in the middle of your lawn. The angel was lying in the grass. All white. About ten inches long, and about five or six inches wide. Oddly enough, there was a string attached to it."

Peyton looked relieved. It hadn't yet dawned on me that she might think I was "seeing things." In earnest, I was puzzled. *Omen? Was something odd about to happen? Was I finally going to encounter a real angel?* I walked to the front door and looked out. Back in the kitchen, I said, "It's gone."

Peyton replied, "Well, the yard guys just left. They must have done something with it."

I shook my head and mumbled out an um-hmm. But why did I feel that something out of the ordinary was in the making?

Later, I headed home across Monteagle Mountain. Sometimes on this leg of my journey, I detoured from the interstate to stop off at Sewanee University. During the holidays beautiful wreaths enhanced the church doors while church bells rang. And the names and dates on the old gravestones in the campus cemetery intrigued me. Whether winter, spring, summer, or fall, the campus was always beautiful. Peaceful. This day, there was low lying fog. Perhaps I wasn't too wise leaving the interstate to drive into the gray-white soup.

A building distracted me from my musings. On the side of the road stood a small establishment that sold pottery. Or claimed to sell pottery. How many times had I passed the place of business wanting to go inside for a peek? But how many times did the place looked closed, as if no lights were on and no cars parked outside. On my way back home I would pull in and see if it were open. For now, I couldn't wait to see how my favorite double doors on the Sewanee campus were decorated. Every year, the wreaths were different. Through the mist, the wreaths I spotted were green, decorated with holiday ribbon the color of subdued earth tones. Beautiful.

Grabbing my iPhone, I jumped out of my car to take a quick photo. That's when I heard music. Bells ringing. I hadn't heard the hymn playing in ages. Stopping long enough to snap a picture, I decided to video the wreaths with the music playing in the background. On the way back to the car, I sang what few words I could remember.

> Angels we have heard on high,
> Singing sweetly o'er the plains

Didn't sound right. Maybe I was throwing some "Star Spangled Banner" or "America the Beautiful" in there. But the chorus I could recall.

> Gloria in excelsis Deo.
> Gloria in excelsis Deo.

At least I recalled the chorus. I'd have to look up the verses when I got home. And what did the Latin word *excelsis* mean? Not only was the mountain foggy, my brain was foggy. Surely I'd known every verse at one time while in the junior choir in church. That was a long time ago.

On the way back to the interstate, there it was. The log cabin with the pottery in the window. No lights. No cars. But there was one sign of life. Smoke curled from a chimney, headed for the heavens. Turning the wheel, I parked in front, then saw someone crack the door open. Taking the gesture as a welcome, I opened the door wider. A guy was on the phone and also trying to turn on lights. He smiled and nodded. "Come on in. I'll get these lights on in a minute."

"Don't mind me," I said. "I'll just take a look around while you're finishing your call."

Before I turned around, the cutest little girl, I guessed to be around ten years of age, popped out from behind another door. With blonde hair, a bright smile, and a willingness to help, she said, "Are you looking for something special?" She pointed out a couple of hand knitted baby hats. One blue striped. In the dim light, one orange looking. *Seriously? Orange for a baby?* Babies usually wore pastel colors. No interest there. "Need a hat for a baby?" she asked.

"I'm just browsing. Besides, my granddaughters are three and almost five." Honestly, I'd already bought Christmas presents and promised myself I was doing nothing more than looking. No more spending. Not one more penny. Celebrating Christmas was always way too expensive. Never knew what the future would bring.

"Those hats definitely wouldn't fit then." The child began pointing out different pieces of pottery. "My mom made these."

Within a few sentences, she shared that her mom was ill with breast cancer. *Christmas. And a child's mother was suffering?* I tried to keep my moans silent and checked my tears. Fought them back. Then couldn't help it — while still browsing — should I ask? "How's your mom doing? Is she better?"

"Mmmm. Not really. The doctors aren't sure if she'll get better. Do you like this bowl? Oh." She took a closer look. "It's a yarn bowl." She pointed out the slit in the side of the bowl where the yarn should be placed to keep from tangling.

"You know, I've been wanting one of those." And I had been. For quite awhile. But for years I'd made do without a yarn bowl while knitting and with yarn bowls being pricey...I did not need a yarn bowl. "What's your Mom's name. I'll be praying for her."

"Shawneeg."

"What an interesting name." I picked up the yarn bowl and gave it a good once over. "I believe I need me a yarn bowl." The child's eyes lit up while a smile covered her face as she directed my attention to more of her mother's pottery. "Are all of these other beautiful mugs and bowls by different potters?"

"Yes," replied the little imp with a laugh. "About eighteen others have their pottery here." With a grin, she motioned me elsewhere. "There's more of

Mom's work in this other room."

"Well, let's go see more of her pieces."

The child's father stepped from an adjoining office and apologized again, this time for the cold room. I knew all about trying to be a good steward of God's money. Saving on electric bills had always been a priority. And besides. It wasn't fair this child's mother was deathly ill. During the week of Christmas. *Cancer. Hospital bills. God, how fair is that? She's just a child. She needs her mother. Please heal her mother.*

"You have quite the little salesgirl here. You might want to let her help all of your customers." The child's father grinned before going back to his phone call.

That's when I saw it. That one piece I might not be able to live without. Before me was a light blue bowl. And in the bottom of the bowl was a raised cross of dark blue glass. The cross. *Christmas. The birthday of Jesus who would die on a cross. Times are probably difficult right now with medical expenses.* No. I couldn't afford anything else. I didn't know what other bills might pop up myself. I'd just had two windfall trees removed from my lawn. Health insurance was out the roof. There was always something. Better not buy another thing.

But that bowl could be such an incredible conversation piece. I imagined a party where people scraped the bottom of the shrimp dip bowl to find, lo and behold, a cross at the bottom. *Just a reality check friends. Ha-ha! Heaven or hell — wanted to make sure my guests are sure of their salvation. Does everyone know where they're going?*

The child before me pointed out another piece as I moved away from the bowl with the dark blue cross. "Oh honey, I'd buy every piece in this shop if I could." She giggled. *How could this precious child laugh when her mother was near death?*

"If you had a thousand dollar discount?"

Then *I* began to laugh. And I was shown more Mom pieces. "Mom said this plate has a mistake in it. She never liked these plates because of the mistakes." The child had become wistful, perhaps thinking about her future without her mother, thinking about what might have been. With a voice tender and sweet she added, "But I think they're pretty."

44

"Mistakes sometimes make the pottery even more special," I replied. "More interesting." I'd thrown a few pieces of pottery on a wheel and knew about mistakes and how to use those mistakes to make a work of art come alive. And functional. Even educational. I once used a vase with a hole in the bottom to teach a children's class at church that like people, even the imperfect can be used. "I think those plates are pretty too, but I *must* have the bowl with the cross inside. And I think that will do me." I had to make my escape before the child talked me into mortgaging my home to buy out the rest of the store.

"Dad, I think she's ready to check out."

"What's your name?" I asked the blonde beauty while I waited on her father to add up my small haul.

"Trinity Grace."

Caught off guard, again, I replied, "That's one of the most beautiful names — ever." If I didn't get out of the store soon, I felt I would burst into tears. Everything about this visit reeked of a God who arranges encounters.

Choking back my emotions, I said, "I'm going to have another granddaughter soon. Her name is Hope."

The child stepped over to the shelf that held the hand knitted baby hats she'd previously tried to sell me. She handed me the orange hat. I said, "Oh no! Don't tell me the hat says Hope on it?" By the sparkle in her eyes I knew I'd guessed at a truth and we laughed. She knew she'd made another sale, because at the top of the hat was a wooden button that indeed had the word Hope on it. "Okay. I have to have it, but is this orange? What color is this, I don't have my glasses on." If I was buying a baby an orange hat what in the world would go with this color? It would have to be a Big Orange baby Hope. Go Vols. My alma mater.

"It's not orange," said Trinity Grace. "It's red."

Adjusting my glasses, I held the hat up to the light. Holy Moly. It had been red all along. "Well, Dad, guess you'll have to ring this sale up as well. Like I said, you need to have your daughter help *all* of your customers. By the way, how's your wife doing. Trinity Grace told me about her cancer."

With measured words, I was told, "We've been to Mayo Clinic recently. That's why we haven't been in the shop lately. The doctors have Shawneeg on medication and she's had treatments but the cancer has gone into her back as well as her brain. We drive to Chattanooga for her treatments now, so that's not as far away."

I assured the man I, and others, would pray for her. Then I asked, "I'm just wondering...it's obvious your wife is a Christian since she put a cross in a bowl before firing it...and I'm wondering if she had an incredible God moment when she came to the Lord? Any special story there?"

"Not really. One thing though, after she'd been working here at Hallelujah Pottery, the owners decided they wanted to move out west. And they made it possible for Shawneeg to take over the business." I'd forgotten about the sign outside. Hallelujah Pottery. Should have been a dead giveaway these people were Christ followers.

"Well, I would say that's definitely a God moment when you get a business handed to you." With that, Trinity Grace reached up to hug me goodbye. She squeezed out a big smile and said, "Merry Christmas." I hugged her back and made my exit before I broke down in one sobbing mess. As I started my car, Trinity stood in the door and waved — still smiling. Then a fiery dart pierced my imaginary shield. Either Trinity Grace and her father were the biggest con artists selling their wares or they were the truest Christians I'd ever met. Smiling in the face of adversity.

Down the mountain, I prayed, "Lord, none of this is fair. What's happening to that child and her mother, and a father who may soon lose the love of his life — none of it is fair! And right here at Christmas." Sometimes, death shows no mercy.

Then it hit me — the hand knitted hat I'd just bought. My unborn granddaughter's full name would be Hope Ruby. The hat, in good light, was a deep ruby red. With a wooden button on top that said Hope. Perhaps earlier, the angel lying on the front lawn did have a message for me after all. The day would be memorable. I would not only be singing about angels, I would be meeting a little angel. Trinity Grace.

When I arrived home, I was shocked to find that someone's vehicle, for the second time, had left the road and torn down a huge section of my four-board fence leaving deep ruts in my pasture. More expense. Good thing I didn't buy out Hallelujah Pottery. This would be a costly repair. *Lord, this is not fair. People destroy my property, leave the scene, and never offer to pay restitution or leave a note to say I'm sorry.*

I was quickly reminded, *For now, you have the money to pay for the damage done, food on your table, and a warm roof over your head, and you're in decent health.*

I got it. Don't sweat the small change. No way was I going to let one more setback get me down. My problems were nothing compared to the young family I'd just met. Then I remembered Gloria in Excelsis Deo — glory in the highest to God — and Googled the lyrics.

> Angels we have heard on high,
> Singing sweetly through the night,
> And the mountains in reply
> Echoing their brave delight.
> Gloria in excelsis Deo.
> Gloria in excelsis Deo.

I'd been to the mountain that day and heard from angels on high. I'd met a brave little girl and her father who echoed the joy of angels on a mountain top they called home — even with death stalking at their door.

> Shepherds, why this jubilee?
> Why these songs of happy cheer?
> What great brightness did you see?
> What glad tiding did you hear?
> Gloria in excelsis Deo.
> Gloria in excelsis Deo.

On the mountain top, I'd heard a song of happy cheer, seen great brightness in the face of a beautiful child with a name that reassured me that the Father, the Son, and the Holy Spirit were all one and full of grace, no matter the crushing situation. No matter the struggle. No matter the timing. But how could these shepherds I'd just met, these bright angels full of glad tidings, be so jubilant and without even mentioning their faith?

Come to Bethlehem and see Him whose birth the angels sing;
Come, adore on bended knee
Christ, the Lord, the new-born King.
Gloria in excelsis Deo.
Gloria in excelsis Deo.

How appropo. In only a couple of weeks, I would be traveling to Israel, and hopefully, I would be able to visit Bethlehem if all went well.

See him in a manger laid
Whom the angels praise above;
Mary, Joseph, lend your aid,
While we raise our hearts in love.
Gloria in excelsis Deo.
Gloria in excelsis Deo.

And before leaving the mountain top, through the purchase of a few functional and lovely items, I'd been able to "lend aid" to a father and his child who were also lending aid to God by raising hearts of love to a perfect stranger therefore raising hearts in love to God, even though their own hearts had been saturated with months of mountainous grief.

What to make of all of this heartache and sadness in hearts that were yet still so exquisitely full of joy-filled pain? Trinity was the perfect example of a Christian bestowed with grace and exuding joy even while living in the valley of the shadow of death.

And in all circumstances, God is still here, provides, and still sends angels, though he is highly likely to send angels in human form to help and encourage one another. And through His sovereign Trinity, grace is enough. Experiencing grace is so much better than any thousand dollar discount.

And in all things, Gloria in excelsis Deo.

Hallelujah and Merry Christmas!

~ Vicki H. Moss

13

Rudolph and I Are Buddies

Good morning, Rudolph. Or maybe you're one of the others. I never can remember all the names. Chalk that up to a grandmother who insisted I memorize the twelve days of Christmas malarkey while my friends ran around singing about flying reindeer. If it makes you feel any better, I don't remember all that partridge in a pear tree stuff either. Anyway, whichever you are, you're a day early."

It was Christmas Eve morning, so early that maybe it was still night. I started down the driveway of our home in Chapel Hill to pick up the newspaper and there he was. I studied the creature standing at the edge of our security light. Tall. A handsome rack perched on his head. A large body supported by four slender legs. His nose wasn't lit up, but maybe that only happens when he leads the pack. Of course, that might be some of Santa's magic.

You're going to tell me this was an ordinary deer, and you could be right. We certainly have enough of them around here. It's common to see as many as eight of the creatures in our yard at any hour of the day or night. The latter plays havoc with our security light (to say nothing of our lawn), but it's fun to see the fawns frolicking around Momma when they think two-legged critters are tucked snugly in bed. I've seriously considered building an outhouse and toilet training them. If I did, walking in our yard would be safer.

So there we stood, staring at each other, Rudolph dressed in fur and I in my husband's ratty old Virginia Tech jacket. It was a standoff.

"Listen, Rudolph," I said in my sweetest, most conciliatory voice. "You can hear my teeth chattering. I expect to turn into an icicle at any moment, so why don't you mosey on along. Santa surely needs you on this day of all days."

He tilted his head as though giving judicious consideration to my request and apparently thought it was reasonable because he turned and ambled across the road and into the woods. "'Ere he went out of sight," I shouted. "Don't forget where I live, Rudolph!"

49

When I told my husband about my little adventure, he threatened to confine me some place where I can't hurt myself or anyone else. I sniffed at the very idea. Jealousy, pure and simple — that's Jim's problem. *He* didn't get to meet Rudolph!

- Peggy Ellis

14

Christmas Star

I'm being interrogated. All eyes are on me. A bead of sweat rolls down my forehead. My fingers clutch the arm of my chair. I am surrounded with every exit blocked…and it's CHRISTMAS!

The scene was not from a movie. It was not from a tour in Iraq. This was the first time I met my girlfriend's parents. My girlfriend Erica and her mom tried to play defense and keep me comfortable, but the dad was a straight shooter and I was the target. He was trying to gauge what my intentions were. The truth was I indeed had intentions. I wanted to marry Erica, and I wanted to get her Father's permission. However, there was a problem. Every guy who had ever been interested in Erica — I mean every single guy — had been told quite directly that he was not the one for Erica. Remember, her father was a straight shooter and he shot the previous guys hopes down quicker than a young kid opens gifts on Christmas morning.

Her father knew that Erica was special and it wasn't just because she was his daughter. Erica was unique. She honored her parents, she was creative and talented, and in my experience had an innocent beauty that seemed to be an endangered species. She loved God and she was quirky cute which I loved. Both her father and I knew Erica was a star. She starred as Belle in the Musical Beauty and the Beast, she starred as a leader and role model in college, heck she even signed her name with a star.

Her father fixed his gaze on me from his leather-bound man chair across the room, and for a moment I thought he knew. I thought he saw right through me and knew, that there was no way on God's green earth that I was good enough for his daughter. She was a star…I was a dreamer hoping her dad would look the other way for just a moment.

The conversation died down, we ate dinner, and carried on a casual conversation, even though deep down I knew it wasn't casual. It was a bit of an interview. Sometime later her dad and I were walking along the Oregon

Beach. I had arranged for us two men to have some free time to talk. I was waiting for the right moment to ask him for his daughters hand in marriage, but I doubted if there would ever be a "right" time.

While I doubted, Dane, her father began to teach me about agates. Agates are unique volcanic rocks that are often found on the coast of Oregon. He was a collector, so he would wake up early in the morning and hunt for these natural beauties. They were important to him, so I listened.

While he talked I prayed. I prayed that he would say yes. I also, asked that God would give me a sign that this was a good time to ask for Erica's hand in marriage. I knew Dane was a spiritual man, so I begged God to give me a miracle. I envisioned all of the other talks he'd had with guys who had wanted to be romantically involved with Erica in the past, and I played out each of the rejections in my mind. Erica honored her parents and wouldn't get married without her father's blessing. She was old fashioned in that way and so was I.

The discomforting mental images, of the heartbroken guys who had gone before me, were interrupted as Erica's Father asked me a question. He asked me if I could find an agate. I knew nothing about agates. In fact, I had never even heard the word until that visit. But as he looked intently at me a wave pushed over our feet and I asked, "Is this one?" And I reached down into the water and sand and pulled out a rock the size of my hand. And in the middle of this smooth white rock was a bit of a translucent side which was in the shape of a star.

I looked at him and he looked at me and we both smiled. In that moment I believed I had gotten my sign, and there was something in his eyes that seemed to say the same thing. I decided to chance it. I opened my mouth and words actually uttered forth, "Dane, I'm going to take this as a sign." I asked him for his star's hand in marriage. He said yes. Some months later, his star became my star. Christmas is my favorite time of year, but there is one Christmas that started off like an interrogation, yet ended up being the one year I will never forget.

- Dr. Jayce O'Neal

15

A Good Eye

The perfect Christmas tree? All Christmas trees are perfect!
— Charles Barnard

Sometimes Grandpa could be as grumpy as a troll.

"Why does it take you so long to get those baking powder biscuits in the oven? My stomach's rumbling," he'd grouse, while Grandma continued to cut out perfect circles of dough with her jelly glass.

"Why do you have to practice right now? You can see I'm taking a nap," he'd grumble from the green velvet parlor sofa. My big sister, Patti, would glance heavenward, and then give me a wink as she quietly turned the lid down over her keyboard.

If I caught him casting a baleful eye my way, I'd quickly set down my "Children's Activities" and scurry to the shed for an armload of split logs to refill the wood box.

But I'll always remember one special December in 1947 when we all lived together in an old Victorian house in Scott Mills, Oregon, and Grandpa began to twinkle like a North Pole elf. He offered to drive us to Salem to pick out a few new Shiny-Brite ornaments at JC Penney. He beamed at Grandma while she treated her fruit cakes to a dousing of brandy and then rewrapped them. He even encouraged Patti to play "Silent Night," which, he told us, came from Austria, just like him.

A few days before Christmas he announced it was time to bring home a tree. My sister and I clamored to accompany him to choose one, but he refused our help.

"I've got a good eye for the perfect tree," he claimed, tossing on his navy plaid Pendleton jacket. "You can trust me. You just start stringing the popcorn, because I'll be back in no time."

We waved goodbye as he nosed his '46 Ford pickup up the hill towards the woods, then headed for the kitchen. The previous afternoon Grandma had popped corn in a kettle, then let it sit overnight to dry out. Now she helped Patti and me thread our needles, and took a nap as we girls spent the afternoon stringing garlands. I slid the berries and popped kernels down each segment of thread, and then Patti tied the segments together. Her long slender fingers were much better at securing the knots.

By the time we'd used every berry and kernel, it was almost dark and Grandpa hadn't yet returned. Grandma went with us outside to drape a few garlands around shrubs and bushes to feed the jays and crows and chickadees. A few fluttered over for a nibble and squawked out their appreciation.

"Don't worry, girls," Grandma said, noticing our worried glances towards the woods. "Grandpa's just taking his time to find the one tree that will be just right."

When he still hadn't appeared by dinner time, Grandma dished up the crusty macaroni and cheese we loved, and we all munched together.

Just before bedtime we heard the pickup sputter up the driveway. We ran outside as Grandpa hopped out and waved a hand toward the bed of the truck.

"It's about eight feet tall, and shaped as pretty as a bell. It's a Noble fir. We'll leave it here for the night and put it up in the morning."

"Grandpa, what took you so long?" I glanced up at the sky. I saw it was so cloudy that Grandpa couldn't have found the North Star if he'd gotten lost.

"It took a little while to find the perfect tree. And this one is. You'll see when we get it up tomorrow."

When Patti and I got to our bedroom and changed into our winter flannel pajamas, she turned to me.

"Don't you know why Grandpa's in such a good mood at Christmas? And why he stayed out so late today?"

I wrinkled my forehead. Was there some mystery here that I hadn't known about? I shook my head.

"Christmas is the one time Grandma doesn't scold him if he drinks a little brandy. Couldn't you smell him when he got home? Didn't you notice how red his face was? He's probably been sitting out in the woods in the cab of his truck singing Christmas songs to himself."

If a nip of brandy made Grandpa more cheerful, it was just fine with me.

Until Christmas Eve my favorite place was right under the tree. After supper I loved to curl up on the soft scarlet chenille blanket Grandma had draped around the stand, and read my magazines and story books. I'd take in the tree's rich piney scent. Then I'd roll over on my back and watch the lights twinkle. I'd pretend I was a woodland creature, a chipmunk or a squirrel, safe and snug, protected by the fir's mighty branches. Sometimes I'd even drift into sleep. Grandma claimed she came into the room once to hear Grandpa and me snorting together like a pair of weary reindeer on Christmas morning.

The night before Christmas Patti played every carol we knew while we sipped hot chocolate and admired the festooned and garlanded tree with its topper light, an angel with gold wire mesh wings and skirt. I think Grandpa had added a little brandy to his cup; his face grew flushed, as Patti had pointed out.

The next morning we opened our presents. Patti and I each received a box of chocolate covered cherries and a bag of peppermints. I got a new baton and Patti a Brownie camera. We both unwrapped a book and a Gibson Girl striped shirtwaist, mine pink, Patti's blue. Santa had been generous.

Patti and I went to the Christmas morning service at the Friends Church. Then that afternoon, after we feasted on turkey and candied sweet potatoes, Patti snapped photos of us all and of our presents. Then I crawled back under the tree. I read the first chapter of my new book, "Dandelion Cottage," and was entranced.

I remember how I rolled over and stared up through the branches of the fir. I took a deep breath of its wonderful aroma, and popped a peppermint into my mouth. I thought about the characters in my book as I listened to Patti, at her piano, sing "Away in the Manger" and "White Christmas." Grandpa snored softly on the sofa.

I realize now that Grandpa indeed had a good eye for a perfect tree. Even though it's true that he reverted to his old grumpy self after New Year's, I've never forgotten that particular tree. Nor those magical days when I lay beneath its boughs where I saw, smelled, heard, touched and tasted…Christmas. That perfect tree was the best Christmas gift ever.

- Terri Elders

16

Christmas Blessing in Checkout Lane 12

It was December 22nd and I stopped at the local grocery store after work to pick up a few items. My stepson was coming for dinner, so I needed to get in and out quickly. I grabbed the tater tots and coleslaw and searched for the quickest checkout lane. It appeared to be checkout lane 12.

I was wrong.

As I stepped into line behind three other people, I spotted an old man standing in front of the credit card reader just ahead. From the confused look on his face and the patient way the young cashier was talking to him, I could tell this might take some time.

The old man looked perplexed. He was clad in wrinkled jeans and a worn black coat. A tattered blue stocking cap covered most of his straggly, gray hair. He wore thick black-rimmed glasses, and when he looked my way, I could see he was missing two bottom teeth. His rough calloused fingers fumbled with the credit card he was holding. He gazed back at the line that had formed behind him and shifted nervously. Appearing lost and confused, he looked to the young cashier for help.

With a calm voice, the cashier directed the man on how to use the credit card reader. From a wrinkled piece of paper in his left hand, the man punched the PIN number in with his right. Upon completion of the transaction, the cashier looked into his eyes and spoke quietly. "Sir, you have a balance of $7.43."

This seemed to throw the old man into a more confused state. "But...the card," he stammered.

"Yes. You used what was on the card, and you still owe $7.43."

The man glanced from the cashier to the line of people behind him and back to the cashier. Before he could speak again, the middle-age man standing behind him looked at the cashier. "May I insert my card?"

"Yes," she said with a smile. "Would you like me to add these other items?"

The middle-aged man nodded.

The cashier rang up two boxes of light bulbs and a couple other items I couldn't see. Apparently, the older man had divided his groceries into two piles. Things he needed and other items he would get if he had enough money.

The cashier finished scanning the items from the second pile and finalized the transaction. The middle-aged man took his card from the reader while the groceries were bagged. With a twinkle in her eyes and a grin on her face, the cashier looked at the old man and said, "You can go now. Your balance has been paid."

Still confused, he asked, "How much did you say I owe? Seven...?"

"You don't owe anything," said the cashier. "This man covered your remaining balance."

The old man gazed back at the other man with a questioning look.

"Merry Christmas, Sir," said the middle-aged man. He smiled.

The older man became still and looked down for a moment. We all stood quietly and watched. When he lifted his head, his face was scrunched and his eyes glistened. He spoke softly. "This is the first Christmas without my wife."

"I'm sorry to hear that."

The old man turned back to the cashier and asked again, "How much did you say I owe?"

In a compassionate voice barely above a whisper she repeated, "Sir, you are free to go. You can leave now. You don't owe anything."

One more time, the old man turned to the middle-aged man. A smile emerged and his eyes sparkled. "You know, for thirty-seven years she was a good wife and mother. But most of all," the old man raised his right hand and patted his chest, "she loved Jesus with all of her heart."

The middle-aged man smiled and extended his right hand. "Merry Christmas, Sir."

The old man's trembling hand grasped the other man's in return and they shook hands. Their hands stayed tightly clasped for a brief moment. Then the old man released his grip and replied, "Merry Christmas." He picked up his bags of groceries and shuffled toward the door.

When the old man was out of sight, the young cashier took a deep breath. She raised her hands and fanned her face to dry the tears that had begun to trickle down her cheeks.

The middle-aged man turned to me and the woman between us. "That's what it's all about, isn't it?" He winked.

With tears in our eyes, we wished each other a Merry Christmas. Then one by one, we completed our transactions and left the store; each of us different than when we entered.

As I left the store with the scene still fresh in my mind, I thanked God for allowing me to be a spectator as this special Christmas blessing unfolded.

It was the most precious gift I received that year. No gift I opened over the next few days would top the Christmas blessing I received in checkout lane 12.

- Sheryl M. Baker

17

A New Song

My favorite Christmas moment did not happen in front of the tree, around the table or at a church service. My favorite moment this particular year was in a hospital room.

My husband's grandmother was not able to come to the family Christmas gathering. She had been ill for several months, but had been declining more rapidly that week. In fact, she had been sleeping the majority of the forty-eight hours before we got there.

What a joy it was to see her wake up to see our three boys. I honestly expected them to stare at her or even look at the floor, because they are not accustomed to hospital beds and medical staff. I thought there was a chance that our four year old would say hello because we have been stressing the importance of good manners.

You can imagine our surprise when he agreed to share his new talent with her. With some encouragement from his daddy, he stood on a chair so she could see his face and whistled an almost perfect "Jingle Bells." And because he couldn't find the courage to try another song, he did "Jingle Bells" again. And again once more.

Grannie's eyes were fixated on this little four year old.

She said he sounded like a bird. I can only imagine that after hearing hospital beeps for several days, bird sounds would be refreshing. For a few minutes, Mason took her to a place of pure innocent joy where she was reminded of the beautiful things in life, the things that will last beyond sickness and pain.

"Jingle Bells" has never made me cry, but it did that day.

It wasn't the song, of course. It was seeing the young with the old, the healthy with the sick, the joy in the sorrow, the smiles through the tears, the peace with the pain.

Isn't that life? Good in the midst of bad.

Mason and Grannie were a beautiful reminder of God's promises. He promises to restore His kingdom, the place where there will be no sadness, pain, or death. We are in a broken place now, but he will make it new.

The goodness here is just a reflection of what is to come.

> Do you not know? Have you not heard? The Lord is the everlasting God, the Creator of the ends of the earth. He will not grow tired or weary, and his understanding no one can fathom. He gives strength to the weary and increases the power of the weak. Even youths grow tired and weary, and young men stumble and fall; but those who hope in the Lord will renew their strength. The will soar on wings like eagles; they will run and not grow weary, they will walk and not be faint. (Isaiah 40:28-31 NIV)

Run and not grow weary.

We knew that was probably the last time we would talk to her, but we left that day with a sense of peace that only God can give. After all, He is the one who made her. She belongs to Him.

We can fully appreciate life when it is slipping away. We grasp the depth of His love during our deepest pain. We are aware of our need for Him upon realizing how little control we have.

Two weeks after Christmas, we celebrated Grannie's life. But more than that, we celebrated the new life that she has found.

The best is yet to come.

- Kristin Tobin Dossett

18

A Gift Unwrapped

My daughter Megan excels at finding the perfect gifts for family and friends, mostly because she listens to what people say about the things that mean a lot to them. So when she told me in September of her sixteenth year that she'd come up with an idea for a special Christmas gift for her father, I couldn't wait to hear about it.

"Mom, you know when Dad tells us about how his father sang 'O Holy Night' every Christmas Eve at their church, we can tell it's a memory he cherishes. Well, I'd like to surprise him by singing it at our Christmas Eve service this year. If I start practicing now, I can be ready by then. What do you think?"

"He would love that," I replied. "You'll need to check with the music director right away. If he's agreeable, then talk with your voice coach and get things rolling."

Megan's brow furrowed, a sign that her planning for this gift had kicked into high gear. "But Mom, please don't tell Dad. I really want to surprise him."

Megan inherited her beautiful voice from her paternal grandfather. Poppy Howerter served the Lord as choir director of his church for nearly half a century. He possessed an exquisite and powerful baritone voice, and every Christmas Eve for forty years, he sang "O Holy Night" at the midnight service. There were many things Tim missed about his beloved father, particularly hearing him sing that song.

Two days later, Megan had the director's approval and began weekly rehearsals with Janet, her voice coach.

Since I always accompanied Megan to her voice lessons, I knew how much work went into singing a song beautifully. A trained vocalist's performance of a difficult song may sound effortless, but many hours of daily practice, usually over a period of weeks, are required to produce it. Week after week, Megan and her coach worked together on the song while I sat in the room listening and taking mental notes of Janet's instruction so I could help Megan when she practiced at home. A recording of Janet playing the song on the studio piano enabled Megan to rehearse at home. During her daily hour-long practices, she frequently asked me to listen and critique her singing as she worked through difficult sections.

She took great care to keep the song a secret from her dad, practicing before he arrived home from work and making sure she kept the sheet music inside her music folder so he wouldn't see it.

Christmas Eve finally arrived and I tried to push my husband to leave the house earlier than we normally would for the late evening service.

"We don't have to leave yet," Tim insisted.

I removed my coat from the closet and slipped it on. "Yes, we do. You know how crowded the church gets."

He remained in his chair. "We can leave in fifteen minutes and still find good seats."

Clearly he wasn't buying my argument.

I turned to Megan and our son Justin who by now was in on his sister's plans and raised my finger to my lips. Turning around, I put my hands on my hips and faced Tim. "All right then, if you must know," I said, using my best guilt-a-person-into-doing-something voice. "I made special arrangements to have one of your Christmas gifts delivered to the church. Now don't make me explain and ruin it. It's all wrapped up and waiting for you, but we need to get there before everyone starts arriving." He didn't know what to say to that, so the four of us got into the car and left.

We arrived at the church before the ushers or anyone else and had the pick of any seat in the sanctuary. "Let's sit up front," I suggested.

Tim shook his head. "We never sit there."

I put on my best smile. "That's true, but for just this once, let's try it."

Justin, Megan, and I started down the center aisle. I didn't look behind me, but I knew Tim followed us. We settled in the first pew and had only been seated a minute when Tim stood.

"Where are you going?" I asked.

He motioned at the lobby. "We didn't get bulletins."

"Oh. That's because they weren't on the table when we came in. They must still be in the office. We'll have to wait until the ushers arrive and start handing them out." I glanced at Justin who knew we didn't want Tim to see a bulletin since Megan's name and the song would be listed in it. "Would you get us bulletins after people start arriving, please?"

He tried not to grin. "Sure, Mom. I'll take care of it."

I turned to Tim. "Why don't you sit and relax?"

"What about my gift?" he asked. "You said there's a gift waiting here for me."

I rested my hand on his arm. "It's here, honey. I didn't see it in the lobby, but it's here. I promise."

Worshipers began filling the sanctuary. Tim leaned across me and whispered to Justin, "Son, if you don't go to the lobby now and get bulletins, there won't be any."

Justin rose from the pew and left. Several minutes later he returned and took his seat. "Sorry, Dad. I waited too long. There are no more bulletins."

Irritation spread over Tim's face, and I knew he suspected nothing. Megan's carefully planned secret gift was still in play.

The service to celebrate the gift of Jesus's birth began. It was beautiful. Each hymn, each scripture paid homage to God's gift of a savior for us. The end of the service neared and only one thing remained before the worshipers sang "Silent Night" and that would be the soloist singing "O Holy Night."

Tim shot me a quizzical look as Megan left our pew and took her place in front of the congregation, a microphone in hand. The organ began the introduction and our daughter's voice took control of the music. Note by note Megan unwrapped the song. Her pure soprano voice delivered the words proclaiming the savior's entrance into the world as she worked her way through the difficult melody with ease.

So intent was I in watching and listening to her sing that I didn't realize my husband was crying until I heard him sniffling. I threw a glance at him. Tears ran down his cheeks.

"What's wrong?" I asked, pulling a handkerchief out of my purse and handing it to him. Tim tried to answer but couldn't. His emotional reaction to our daughter singing a song that meant so much to him made me cry.

After the service ended and people began leaving the sanctuary, Tim looked at me, tears still flowing. "That was the gift, wasn't it?"

I nodded, wiping my eyes. "Yes. It was Megan's idea."

He gazed at her, his voice choking. "You remembered about my dad singing…"

Megan beamed. "Every year you tell us how Poppy sang it on Christmas Eve for forty years and that you loved listening to him sing it. I thought it would be special for you to hear me sing it."

Tim reached out and drew her close to him. "Thank you." He opened his other arm and pulled Justin and me close in a family hug. Our precious Megan, in using her godly gifts of careful listening, thoughtfulness, and song, created a Christmas memory that night each of us will long remember and treasure.

~ *Cynthia Howerter*

19

When Christmas Comes in January

Going into the Christmas season this year, I had to keep in mind that Christmastime is a magical time of year filled with wonder and joy and new beginnings. I had just lost my husband of forty-seven years the month before, and the bright lights of Christmas seemed dim and unimportant. I settled in for a blue Christmas. It was going to be tough, but I had my children. They would be home for the holidays.

When my son and daughter arrived on Christmas morning and I heard, "Mom, we're home! Merry Christmas!" a cascade of forty-seven white Christmases came flooding back. The lights of Christmas suddenly became brighter.

I've always loved Christmas mornings. And even though my children are well into adulthood, Santa Claus still visits their childhood home, placing presents under the tree and helping himself to a handful of freshly-baked cutout cookies — some in the shape of Santa himself.

Their father would sit quietly and proudly next to the tree with its twinkling lights and watch as shiny red bows were ripped from their packages, revealing surprises Santa had left under the tree's branches the night before. Over the years, these presents grew in stature from picture books and tricycles, to CD players and ten-speed bikes, and eventually to used cars and U.S. Savings Bonds to help with college. But whether it was a picture book with Winnie-the-Pooh on its cover or a Savings Bond with George Washington imprinted on it, the delightful sounds of Christmas found their way to their father and the twinkling lights of the Christmas tree.

Family time. Merry Christmases. Beautiful memories.

When it came time to put the decorations and ornaments away, I wrapped each one in tissue paper and placed them in their respective boxes. But I was not quite ready to say good-bye to the tree. Not yet. I wanted to leave it standing for a few more weeks. I welcomed its peaceful presence.

Every January for a number of years now, I've headed to the hospital for my annual, follow-up testing for breast cancer. This January would mark a huge milestone for me. Subsequently, I made an appointment with my surgeon for the physical exam and the reading of the test results. I held my breath....

"No traces of breast cancer," he said. "See you next year."

My heart danced with unbridled joy. Cancer free! Twenty-one years! Leaving his office, I could have flown down three flights of stairs to the main floor, but instead pressed the down button of the elevator.

Making my way to the hospital's exit, I noticed a man coming toward me carrying dozens of balloons in each hand. Balloons of all colors, sizes, and shapes, all reaching for the ceiling. Big ones. Small ones. Round ones. Oval ones. Balloons of every color of the rainbow.

"What a beautiful sight!" I exclaimed, moving out of his way. The man smiled at me and kept walking through a set of double doors; he and the balloons filling up the entire space. I stood next to the wall and watched as this parade of pure merriment marched down the hospital's long corridor.

I wonder where he's going with all those balloons? I asked myself. *What's he going to do with all that excitement? Who's he going to give all that joy to?* I thought about that man and his colorful balloons all the way home.

I woke up the next morning and began my day as usual, but I couldn't get the man and his myriad of balloons out of my mind. Why was I still thinking about all this? I even recalled the light-blue T-shirt and jeans the man was wearing. And his gold-rimmed eyeglasses that reflected the lights from the fixtures above.

As the day wore on and the afternoon shadows melted into evening's twilight, I made a decision. I decided that *this* man, *those* balloons, and *that* celebration of joy were meant for me. A sign from someone somewhere beyond the clouds reminding me that Christmas is a magical time of year filled with wonder and joy and the promise of new life...even when it comes in January.

~ *Lola Di Giulio De Maci*

20

The Offhand Christmas

Though it was still a week until Christmas, I'd already addressed and mailed the cards, bought the tree, and hidden away family presents in a closet that my husband never looked in.

"For once it's under control," I'd congratulated myself, as Ken and I headed for bed. On Saturday I'd shop for a turkey, pick up oranges and cranberries for relish, and bake pecan tassies. Ken enjoyed the tasty tarts, and I could squish together margarine, cream cheese and flour and press it into the mini-muffin tins a lot more easily than I could roll out a perfect pie crust.

Ken's son, Rick, and his wife Angela, would arrive Christmas Eve, and we'd spend the holiday walking the dogs in the snow, playing hearts, and listening to holiday music, enjoying what we deemed our traditional family fest.

I'd hoped to fall asleep quickly, but winds whistled around the windows, and I covered my head with my pillow. I heard banging, and remembered that I hadn't checked if all the doors had been locked before we came to bed, nor had I counted cats. We had three, and in winter we sometimes experienced menacing overnight temperature drops.

I crept out of bed, and started down the stairs. About the third step down my right foot landed on Harpo, my marmalade cat. Before I could grab the railing, I tumbled, head first, throwing out my left arm to break my fall. I landed, stunned, at the foot of the stairs, but when I finally struggled to my feet I suspected I'd sustained a serious injury. My left arm hung limply by my side and my shoulder felt lumpy.

I dragged back upstairs and woke Ken.

"I doubt anything's broken," he said. "It's probably a sprain. What were you doing wandering around in the dark?"

"I thought I heard the screen door banging. I wanted to make sure the cats were all inside. Then I stepped on Harpo. He blended in with the carpet."

"If you still think something's wrong when the sun comes up, I'll drive you to the hospital. Try to get some sleep. I wish the winds would die down."

I flopped down on my right side and drifted off, despite my throbbing arm and the howling winds.

By dawn my arm had swollen to twice its normal size. Ken drove me to the hospital. The ER doctor said x-rays revealed that the ball of my shoulder had been knocked out of its socket and sustained multiple fractures. He'd schedule surgery. My arm would be immobilized in a sling for several weeks. If no complications developed, I possibly could return home by Christmas Eve.

Ken listened patiently to my concerns prior to the operation. He'd undergone a quadruple bypass eight months earlier, so I worried about the strain on him of trying to take care of the cats, dogs…and me.

I nattered on about Christmas, how I still had gifts to wrap, groceries to buy, tarts to bake, floors to mop, and tables to dust. With an immobilized arm, how would I even bathe, dress and feed myself? I'd heard the old joke about people who broke a hand, wrist or shoulder the week or so before Christmas in order to avoid kitchen duty. Not funny.

"Calm down," Ken finally said. "I'll take care of everything. I'm not incapable, you know."

The surgery went well, so on Christmas Eve the doctor discharged me with a long list of do's and don'ts, heavy on the latter.

Once at home, I again peppered Ken with my worries:

"How will I wrap the presents? What about tinsel? The tassies? Oh, no, we didn't buy a turkey. There might not be any fresh ones left at the market and it's too late to thaw one."

"All taken care of," Ken said, with an assertive nod. "We've got ribeyes in the freezer and I'll barbecue. I'll stick some potatoes in the oven, along with a frozen apple pie, and we've got plenty of salad makings. Now stop worrying."

"The tinsel? The presents?"

"The tree has plenty of ornaments. It doesn't need any tinsel. Stuff the gifts in bags and stick a label on the outside. We don't need ribbons and foil."

I glowered, but grabbed a fistful of grocery sacks and a pad of labels and headed to the closet where I'd stashed the gifts. I'd ordered most of the presents online, since we lived far from any department stores. Luckily, I'd opened the boxes as they'd arrived. I never could have managed now with just one hand. My forehead wrinkled with regret as I plopped each gift into a plastic carrier bag. I hoped the recipients would forgive their appearance. I scrawled names on stickers and slapped them on the sacks. Thank heavens my right hand worked all right.

They sure don't look like Christmas presents, I thought, as I dragged the bags to the tree.

On Christmas morning Ken helped me open the fancy packages that Rick and Angela had brought. We joked about the grocery bags but agreed this was an environmentally green effort, since we'd recycle the bags, rather than shove them in the rubbish bin.

It indeed had snowed and we took the dogs for their morning frisk. This time Ken held the Akita's leash. Later we played our traditional hearts game, even though it took some time for me to sort out my cards and arrange them in order with only one hand. When it was my turn to deal, Rick dealt for me.

In the late afternoon as the sun began its descent, Ken and Rick fired up the barbecue and set the table. Angela tossed a salad and chopped green onions to top the baked potatoes. Then we took our usual seats and Ken carried in his ribeyes from the grill. Everybody else dug in. I picked up my fork and stared at my plate.

I decided to adopt a light note.

"How am I going to eat this? Do I pick up the whole thing in my hand and start to gnaw? Do I lean down like the dogs and nibble around the edges?"

After they all shared a hearty laugh at my quandary and Rick had said grace, Ken cut my steak into bite-sized chunks, added a dollop of sour cream to my potato, and filled my salad plate. He did everything but spoon-feed me my slice of pie.

The trio even cleared the table and washed the dishes while I sat in the living room in front of the tinsel-free tree, reviewing the day as I sipped a nightcap of mulled wine.

The snowy stroll, free from a two-handed struggle to restrain a one-hundred fifteen-pound Akita, the slower-paced card game which provided more time to chat, the novelty of a Christmas barbecue, and watching my capable Ken take charge...I'd been delighted by it all.

I soon went to bed, still weak from trauma and surgery, but glowing with contentment. Ken was right. Christmas needs neither flashily wrapped gifts nor the shimmer of a tinseled tree...not even the tang of cranberry relish, nor the scent of a roasting turkey. Christmas just needed us, willing to share its timeless message of peace.

~ Terri Elders

21

Love Notes in the Snow

The mid point of December had arrived and though the thermometer on the front porch hovered close to twenty degrees, the sun glowed high in the sky and the crisp clean air offered all the invitation I needed. So I threw on my parka, pulled Daddy's work gloves and pruning sheers from the shed, and started the trek up the side of Cinder Hill in the direction of the pines.

As I neared the group of trees, that this year would sacrifice a bough or two for my annual Yule Tide decorations, I thought back on the Christmases when my parents were newly retired. Though well into their sixties then, they still delighted in the scent of a freshly cut pine tree for Christmas. The ones they chose were never more than three or four feet tall, but the size of the tree didn't matter much to them, only that the scent of pine should emanate from it. Those were wonderful years for Mom and Dad, free from pain and sickness. Free from the maladies that eventually left me a forty-six-year-old orphan.

When I am out in our back yard, my thoughts often turn to the memories of how my parents loved and respected nature. They gardened meticulously and spent countless hours appreciating the beauty of watching flower and vegetable gardens grow. But their love of nature did not end there. From the time I was a child every dog in the neighborhood knew their way to our house where Daddy doled out soup bones he'd pick up at the super market. Meanwhile, Mom built a career out of feeding the sparrows.

As I pruned several large branches and carried them down the hill to our patio, these memories ran through my mind like long lost home movies. At Christmas, my heart aches for my parents.

On the patio, I cut the boughs down further and worked the smaller pieces through the wire wreath form I had purchased the day before. For the bow, I chose a wide white ribbon decorated with vibrant red poinsettias and brilliant green holly leaves. Holly and poinsettias ranked high on Mom's list of favorite Christmas symbols. When finished, I loaded the wreath into the car to deliver it the following day.

A light snow fell overnight but by noon the warmth of the sun had eliminated every trace of it on the streets and sidewalks so I ventured out and drove to the cemetery. It didn't occur to me to wear boots since our sidewalks and streets were clear and dry. But as I drove through the gates and headed down the winding road that leads to our family plot, I noticed the snow throughout the graveyard hadn't melted.

Having reached Saint Matthew Avenue, I parked to the side of the road and lifted the wreath from the back seat. When I stepped out of the car the chilly wind that pricked at my skin made me wish I'd considered a hat and scarf in addition to boots.

I trudged toward the oh-so-familiar headstone where my grandparents and now my own parents lay in rest. Everywhere I looked a pristine blanket of white stretched out before my eyes dotted with granite and marble grave markers. Each one paid tribute to loved ones who left behind a family to carry on, armed only with the comfort of their treasured memories. A gray cloud of sadness settled over me.

The snow, deep enough to clear the top of my sneakers, crept over the sides, getting my socks sopping wet. I plodded on, shivering and annoyed at myself for being so unprepared. The wind grew stronger and gnawed at my nose and cheeks while my mood soured with every step. Why wasn't I more prepared? Why hadn't I thought this through? And while we're at it, why did Mom and Dad have to die in the first place?

At last I reached my destination. When I looked down to put the wreath in place I stared in disbelief at the site that lay before me. Though not another human footprint pierced the snow anywhere around that grave, tiny bird tracks and canine paw prints clearly chiseled a path directly in front of the Tait headstone.

For a moment I was not alone in my grief for the loss of Mom and Dad. There in the snow before me was all the proof my heart needed that they were loved and missed by more than just me.

I left the cemetery with a much lighter heart. With my newfound joy came the determination to feed the sparrows when I got home, and find a good soup bone for my dog. That seemed a proper way to say thank you and earn smiles of approval from Mom and Dad.

Amazing! Just as I had left a wreath to express my feeling for Mom and Dad, even the small creatures of God's animal kingdom had left a love note in the snow.

- Annmarie B. Tait

22

The Christmas Wish Books

I love to peruse catalogs, especially during the holiday season. I enjoy looking at those specialty items not seen throughout the year. They come from every corner of the United States. I used to receive dozens of wish books each year and I'd go through them, page by page, and remember holidays past and hopes for the future.

My dreaming started in 1950 when my younger sister and I waited for the mailman to deliver our JC Penney and Sears, Roebuck and Company Christmas Wish Books. When they arrived, we sat for hours, examining each page, finding it hard to make a decision on what we wanted Santa to bring. Finally, with a crayon, we circled our favorite items and hoped Mom would see and let Santa know.

Catalog dreaming carried over into my adult life. I live in the high desert. December without snow is something I've lived with all my life. Catalogs brought the beautiful winter season into my home and I would find myself dreaming of a white Christmas.

In the evening after I put the children to bed, I sat in my lazy chair, grabbed a cup of hot brewed Sleepytime tea and imagined to my heart's content. There is something special about a tour through a Holiday Book. None of that internet-scrollin' through stuff for me. I turned the pages with my fingers.

For several years I knew I would not be going "home for the holidays." So, the catalogs set the scene of enticement and excitement for my seasonal plans. The planning was more important than the shopping. The anticipation was like preparing for a vacation.

I opened the book and took a tour through the culinary section which invited me to breathe the aroma of spiced apple cider brewing in a red crock pot, for $29.99. Gingerbread man cookie cutters tempted my thoughts of baking cookies. The gorgeous table settings were ready for my family to sit down and enjoy their holiday meal. There were elegant table runners, linen or lace table cloths, place mats and napkins, all to match, and in a choice of colors.

Centerpieces of evergreen garlands gracefully lay down the middle of the table along with red poinsettias placed around glass candlesticks. The vintage inspired gold rimmed china, or fashionable stoneware place settings, goblets and glasses, were mine at the available low cost, plus shipping.

I turned to page twelve and imagined myself decking the halls with boughs of holly with fresh fir evergreen and pinecone garlands around the staircase rails. On the fireplace mantel were sprays of fragrant pine conifer, tall sterling silver candlesticks and red and gold glass bulbs, finished with red bows. I took a trip down memory lane with the colorful bubble candle lights.

Pine greenery and dried grape vine wreaths were ready to embellish my front door for $32.50. Red artificial poinsettia bouquets of various sizes and prices were available.

The catalog always displayed an overstuffed chair sitting by a crackling fire in the old stone fireplace, while the family dog snoozed on a comfy rug. I imagined seasonal music playing "Chestnuts Roasting on an Open Fire." Hanging stockings A, B, C or D, ready for Saint Nicholas to fill, cost only $19.99.

Do you see Santa wondering how he is going to come down the chimney with a blazing fire?

Of course not! He will come through a window.

What would Christmas be without a horse drawn sleigh trotting through the winter wonderland's cold, glistening white snow. I could hear sleigh bells ring and it seemed someone asked, "Are you listening?"

My heart responded, "Yes, I'm listening and I hear jingle bells."

I imagined me, sitting in the middle of the sleigh, all wrapped up in a wool blanket that cost only $89. I wore a crocheted hat, and a fur lined nylon jacket zipped up to my chin. Paying $125 was a small price for having Jack Frost nipping at my nose. The snow laden tree branches set the pristine mood of elegance. I was on a trip over the river and through the woods to grandmother's house when I passed Frosty the Snowman.

And last, at the back of the catalog, came the nativity section which reminded me of whose birthday we were celebrating.

I had my choice of small tabletop settings, or larger scenes for my front porch or lawn. The catalogue advertised that size didn't matter because they had whatever I wanted. There were porcelain, wood, and molded sets. All priced accordingly, you could have a fifteen-piece set or a smaller arrangement.

Then, I noticed an advertisement reading, Special Purchase: Order Today. The display next to the sign showed a 6" statue of Santa Claus, dressed in his red suit with a black belt, hat trimmed in white fur, and black boots. Santa was kneeling on one knee and praying over the baby Jesus, wrapped in swaddling blankets and lying in a hay-lined manger.

I was in awe. This little statue spoke volumes to my heart regarding the holidays and my biblical perspective of the season. Santa can come, and we can celebrate Jesus' birth. When we share our love through gifts and time with our family and friends, we demonstrate the love Jesus has for the world.

I closed the Christmas Wish Book that is filled with some of the most gorgeous decorations any family would love to have in their home for the holidays.

Guess who was on the back cover? Rudolph the Red Nosed Reindeer and his pals flying away with Santa Claus waving a white gloved hand saying, "I Wanna Wish You a Merry Christmas from the Bottom of My Heart."

I received only ten catalogues last Christmas season. Eventually, they will become obsolete.

However, my enthusiasm for the commercial advertising through the Christmas catalogues can't hold a candle to the beauty of a Christmas Eve Candlelight Service where friends and family come together, united as one, to celebrate the birth of our Savior and to sing "Silent Night" and "Joy to the World."

- Gayle Fraser

23

Messengers of Mercy

It was 1945 and my aunts, uncles, and cousins had come to our house for the annual Thanksgiving dinner. Towering snowdrifts and frosted pumpkins outside the dining room window reminded me that Christmas was right around the corner. I could hardly wait. I was five years old.

After dinner, my sister, cousins, and I were playing in the basement when I fell off a twelve-inch-high step stool onto my back.

"Mom, Lola isn't moving!" my sister yelled, as she ran upstairs to the kitchen to get Mom.

Mom helped me up the steps and sat me on a chair. Noticing that I was turning yellow and blue, she quickly wrapped me in a blanket and got my Uncle Paul to take me to Mercy Hospital in his car. Mom, Dad, and I sat in the back seat, watching the windshield wipers work overtime, swishing clumps of snow from one side of the window to the other.

Several doctors met us in the emergency room when we arrived. The doctors, machines, and lights frightened me. And to add to my heightened fear, my mom and dad were not permitted to stay in the emergency room with me. Hospital practices were different back then.

Mom had worn her heavy tweed coat to the hospital. As I lay on the examining table, I soon realized that if I threw my head back far enough, I could see her coat draped over a chair behind me. I knew that my mom would never leave me without putting her coat on. It was too cold outside.

In the midst of trying to diagnose my condition, the doctors were abruptly interrupted when a tall, young intern — uninvited and unannounced — entered the room.

"It's her spleen. She's ruptured her spleen. It has to come out. STAT!"

No one questioned the intern's diagnosis. No one asked his name or why he was "on duty" that night. He simply appeared out of the blue.

One of the doctors immediately turned to my mother. "Who's your surgeon? We'll call him."

"I don't have a surgeon," Mom said. "Wait a minute! I was on the city bus a couple of weeks ago. Two women were sitting in the seat behind me talking about this surgeon who had the gift of God in his hands. Doctor Harold. Yes! That was his name. Doctor Harold."

The hospital got in touch with him immediately.

"Twenty minutes and it would have been too late," someone said.

What seemed like a minute and an eternity later, I woke up in an all-white hospital room with a big white bandage across my abdomen. Throughout the three weeks I lay there in that hospital bed rallying for my life, nurses in white uniforms and white caps wandered in and out of my room. I wasn't as afraid when they were there. And besides, Christmas was coming, and I was the kid with the "Countdown to Christmas" calendar. I didn't want to miss Christmas. Santa always found my house, even when there was a lot of snow on our roof. I had to be there, waiting for him, in my own bed.

As I got stronger, the nurses let me be a little girl, encouraging me to play. Someone had given me a tube of red lipstick, which I used generously to adorn my lips, my cheeks, and the white sheets and pillowcases. When my mom noticed the red ribbons of color splashed everywhere, she apologized profusely to the nurses.

"Let her have fun," they insisted.

"Angels of mercy," Mom called them.

A little before Christmas, I was well enough to leave the hospital. I lay in the backseat of the car, watching the city's bright lights twinkle off and on in their Morse Code fashion. I was sure they were wishing me a "M-e-r-r-y C-h-r-i-s-t-m-a-s." I could hardly wait to get home. Santa had promised me a doll.

My family greeted me as I was carried through the front door into the living room. I felt as though I had been away forever, but the first glimpse of the sparkling lights and silvery tinsel on the Christmas tree made me feel better.

I was finally home.

And best of all, on Christmas morning, I got my doll. She wore a red-and-white polka-dotted dress with a bonnet to match. She was almost as big as I was. She had been waiting for me under the tree.

Many Christmases have now come and gone. Once in a while I think back on that snowy Thanksgiving Day in 1945, and I wonder....

Who was that young, larger-than-life intern who appeared out of the blue that cold Thanksgiving night when a diagnosis was so desperately needed to save my life? Who were those two women on their way to wherever, talking about a surgeon who had the gift of God in his hands?

Perhaps they were messengers of mercy who didn't want to disappoint a little girl who kept a countdown calendar to Christmas — a little girl who dreamed of a doll with a red-and-white polka-dotted dress and a bonnet to match.

- Lola Di Giulio De Maci

Tradition

The stockings all hung by the chimney with care in hopes that Saint Nicolas soon would be there.

I'm smiling because this is a tradition that is ongoing with our family. Only now, the stockings hang from southwestern ladders.

All my children are grown. I have a daughter in Texas with three grown grandchildren, son and wife in Cave Creek, Arizona, and a daughter in Cottonwood, Arizona. Since we are a bit scattered, our goal each Christmas is to gather together for rekindling old memories, laughing 'til our bellies hurt, and opening our stockings.

We decided some years ago that we didn't need to exchange presents. Some of us were flat-out broke, and others didn't need something new to dust, nor have time to stand in a store's return line.

We started a new tradition. We would collect $20 from each participant and go to breakfast on Christmas morning, then leave a sizable tip for the server who had to work on a day when most are off. We all leave feeling really good, especially when we can't get out of the restaurant quick enough and the servers run us down; tears streaming down their cheeks. Often, we hear stories like, "I can't believe you did this. I didn't have the money to buy my children anything and now I do."

After breakfast, we return to a designated home with a good attitude, surround ourselves with homemade cookies and chocolates while my son distributes each person's stocking.

We draw names early in the year and we put a thirty-dollar limit on gifts. I know, you may ask, "What could you possibly buy in numbers for that amount of money?"

That is the fun part because it isn't the gift, but it's knowing the personality of the receiver and whether individually wrapped favorite candy bars will bring hoots and hollers. You get the idea.

Most Christmas mornings there are at least twelve of us. The routine begins with each person being asked to unwrap a single package from his or her stocking. With so many people, this consumes most of a morning. We laugh, we cry, we reminisce, but most of all we are thrilled to be together for another year.

Our tradition ends with a beautifully prepared dinner from lots of helping hands, card games, and a completed wooden puzzle. The stockings are collected, stuffed in a box and await Saint Nicolas's arrival the next year.

I'm left with a warm fuzziness of tradition that lasts until the following Christmas.

~ Alice Klies

A Father Who Never Leaves

I love you." His voice reassured as he tenderly kissed my forehead.

That was hopeful imagination about my biological father. A girl could dream, couldn't she? In reality, my being so young when he left, and the passing of time, had a way of causing memories to escape. I had forgotten what he was like.

My mother and father grew up in Big Stone Gap, Virginia, a small town nestled in a valley surrounded by the Appalachian Mountains and known for historical museums and coal mining. After a courtship, they married on Christmas Day and moved to El Paso, Texas, where my dad served in the U.S. Army at Fort Bliss.

And then she was pregnant. Surprise! There were two! My twin sister and I made an early appearance and spent weeks in a neonatal ward. Then came double bottles, double diapers, double everything — including double trouble. As toddlers, we often scampered in opposite directions, giving our mom a work-out she didn't sign up for.

When we were about four, our parents parted ways. We stayed with Mom. Then the summer before second grade, my mom scooped everything up — including us — and moved back to her hometown to live with her parents.

My grandfather bought and sold scrap metal at a junk yard he owned at the bottom of the hill, visible from their house. A long, curvy, uphill driveway led to their home.

Childhood memories linger with the trek up and down the driveway by foot or bicycle, catching the school bus, and going to the junk yard to see my grandfather. My grandmother spent a lot of time in the kitchen and had snacks ready when we came in from playing.

Soon we were fortunate to have a wonderful stepfather come into our lives — a man who, along with my mother, cared for and loved us as if we were his own daughters. I am grateful for him.

But line seven of my birth certificate held a different name.

My birth certificate from The Bureau of Vital Statistics, Texas Department of Health, lists the father's name first, directly following my name. That piece of paper was filed, proving my existence by documenting birth and the names of my mother and father. There are no blank spaces.

Yet, my life held a blank space and my heart an empty place — the space meant for a biological father.

I wanted to know my father and be known by him, and be Daddy's girl. I wondered if I could sit on his lap or if he wore cologne. Maybe he would hoist me to his shoulders so I had a better view of animals at the zoo.

And I wondered, *Am I lovable?* If so, why wasn't my father around? I had a loving stepfather. Yet my heart whispered, "A real father stays."

The man listed on my birth certificate came back into my life when I was in elementary school. He gained visitation rights of every other weekend with me and my sister.

My dad became known to me. He liked westerns and Johnny Cash. He cracked open pecans and salted them before eating. Fried bologna and onion sandwiches were a favorite. He played the piano and harmonica. He turned the lights out and told ghost stories. He planned outings for our visits. A lover of history, he took us to historical sites and occasionally a walk through old cemeteries. I didn't care for that activity.

And he trained dogs to guard the several businesses he launched. He gardened and made his own salsa. He loved cars and driving fast. He was a handsome man that women noticed when he entered a room.

One thing he didn't do was take us to church. A self-proclaimed atheist, he'd say, "People think there is a God, but there isn't."

At sixteen, I attended a church service and heard the gospel message: Jesus Christ, sent by His Father, died on a cross for me and loved me completely.

There was the love I craved. I became a daughter of the Heavenly Father. I was no longer a spiritual orphan, but was Daddy's girl in the truest sense. I was a princess, a child of the King!

That day, I began praying for my dad to believe in God — to believe in love. Sixteen years later, it wasn't Father's Day on the calendar, but what a wonderful father's day it was! Party balloons and family members lined the walls of the nursing home's activity room. My dad's mother celebrated her 99th birthday. She believed in God. Both of my grandmothers possessed a strong faith.

During the festivities, my dad approached me teary-eyed. "Did you hear the news?" he said. "I became a Christian."

What I hoped and prayed for had happened. My father accepted the message of the cross. My 16-year prayer was answered. He lived his later years serving God.

In 2010, five days before Christmas, my father passed away. The holidays were bittersweet. The family would not be going to his home for our traditional Christmas night Mexican feast. A lover of spicy food, he started the tradition years earlier knowing his children and grandchildren were ready for a change from the usual holiday foods.

Now my father was having his own feast and celebration in heaven. The image was sweet. The man listed on line seven of my birth certificate was in the presence of my Heavenly Father and *his* Heavenly Father. His birth and name are documented in the Lamb's Book of Life.

Earthly fathers can abandon us, physically or emotionally. Some people will never know their biological fathers. But regardless of our earthly father-child experience, it doesn't compare with our experiences with God the Father. He is best qualified to occupy our blank spaces and empty places with His love and presence. He loved us so much he sent his son in the form of a baby — a baby whose birth we celebrate at Christmastime.

"I love you," Calvary's cross reassures as God tenderly kisses our forehead. He is a Father who never leaves.

~ Karen Friday

26

Is That All?

Afriend and I were talking before our Serendipity Small Group Bible Study began. She asked what my "newest project" was. I enthusiastically responded that I was writing some articles concerning Christmas memories and asked if she had any such memories.

She never hesitated and began sharing as if she were performing on stage in a Dickens's classic which had a lesson for the ages. The following is her story:

"When my daughter was six, she shocked me one Christmas morning. Her father and I had divorced when she was three and a half. As a result, she had two Christmases every year, one with each of us, meaning she received a ton of presents. To her, this was a normal happening because she was so young when her father and I separated.

So after unwrapping all of her gifts on Christmas morning, she looks up at me. Keep in mind that she is completely surrounded by gifts and discarded wrapping paper. So as she looks up at me, she says, 'Is this all?'

I was stunned, saddened and disappointed all at the same time. Looking back, I immediately knew in my heart we needed to make Christmas less about getting and more about giving. I said to my daughter, 'We're going to change our Christmas gift tradition. From now on, we will pick out only one gift. Then we'll use the money that we would have spent on more gifts to adopt a family that needs help with Christmas.'

She seemed to mull it over in her little mind. Granted, she didn't throw a hissy-fit and never really protested, but on the other hand she didn't say it was a great idea either.

As the next Christmas quickly approached, we each had to decide what our one-and-only-one special gift would be for ourselves. We found our perfect family to minister to. It meant there would be many gifts to buy and a lot of plans to make.

Each day God blessed us more than we imagined. My daughter really got into the shopping part of picking out meaningful presents for each child, purchasing and wrapping them.

Unfortunately, my daughter and I had a scheduling conflict that first year. I regret that she was unable to experience the laughter, tears, and hugs of gratitude from the children she had shopped for. At times they were literally breathless as they unwrapped gifts of baby dolls, basketballs, sparkling jewelry, bicycles, skates and lots and lots of new clothes for school. We had even purchased a gift card from a local grocery store for their mother. It was an amazing, never-to-be-forgotten experience.

As I began to leave, the mother of these four small children could not stop crying and hugged me. I was disappointed that my daughter wasn›t able to personally see our initial 'New and Improved Giving Christmas' but when we got together later that evening I enthusiastically shared every single detail.

My daughter and I continued to celebrate our new Christmas tradition for the next ten years, until she left for college. Each year seemed to be a bigger and better experience! Memories that neither of us will ever forget.

I too have been so blessed to see my daughter mature into a beautiful young woman who would rather give than receive.

I thank God for my daughter's asking, 'Is that all?' on that Christmas morning years ago. God touched both our lives when we truly realized that it is more blessed to give than to receive. After all, that's what our Heavenly Father did when He gave his Son to us."

- Tommy Scott Gilmore, III

27

A Lasting Transition... hmm, Tradition

Thanks be to God for his indescribable gift!
2 Cor. 9:15 NIV

Yes, but what about our traditions? I thought, as holiday plans were being made. *Don't they count?*

Thankfully, I put my feelings aside and kept those questions to myself — not something I usually do. We were discussing when, where, and how we would spend Christmas as a family.

Family. Oh, how the meaning of that word changes when you get married. When your kids get married. When your kids have kids. It becomes an ever-evolving cycle. It's not that change is bad, it's just difficult and all parties must be willing to bend.

Traditions are wonderful, but even the best of them have a shelf life. No matter how much we want things to stay the same, life happens and we find ourselves moving in different directions, trying to keep the flame alive.

I remember waking early on Christmas morning as a child in my grandparents' home in South Carolina and running to see what was under the tree. Mama and Papa were always waiting for me with breakfast, hot chocolate, and all sorts of goodies. They made everything special, and I could never imagine spending Christmas anywhere but with them.

After moving to Florida, getting married, and starting my own family, my life was drastically altered. The first Christmas morning in my Tampa home was going well until missing my grandparents got the best of me. I cried. My husband consoled. I cried more. Change and compromise had begun in our household.

As time progressed, my husband and I started taking turns with our plans for the holidays. Some holidays were spent with my grandparents, while others were spent with his parents in Florida. Once we had children, we established traditions in our own home. Eventually, we moved back to South Carolina, my grandparents passed away, and my children got married and started their own families. Once again, I found myself taking turns, doing what everyone else wanted to do.

Even after all these years, there's a small part of me that still wants "MY turn," but I've learned it's far better to be flexible and avoid arguments and hard feelings that would put a damper on our time together. Now, I'm happy with whatever works best for everyone — time spent as a family on Christmas Eve, breakfast on Christmas morning, or a big dinner Christmas afternoon. One year we made plans to go to the Dixie Stampede in Pigeon Forge, but ended up camping in a muddy North Carolina campground.

We've done it all, and it still changes from year to year. You could say our traditions are in a continual state of transition. But as long as it works, I refuse to complain. Being with family is worth whatever sacrifices need to be made.

The important thing to remember is that it's not about *where* you spend the holidays or *when* you get together. It's about *how* you celebrate them. It's not about the food, gifts, or decorations. It's not about whose home or what time of day. Christmas music, eggnog, and stockings hung by the fire are empty and meaningless without the love of family and friends, and the real reason for the season — Jesus Christ, born in a smelly stable as the greatest gift to all mankind. Jesus, King of Kings and Lord of Lords — a tradition engraved in our hearts that will last forever.

- Andrea Merrell

28

A Stroll to Remember

"Every year, the merchants of Red Lodge sponsor a Christmas stroll with free food and entertainment," my sister said over the phone. "The stroll is the first weekend in December. Why don't you and Larry come over?" Since my husband and I were newcomers to the Montana area, my sister kept us abreast of the local activities.

Bundled up for the bracing winter weather, we drove the twenty-five miles across the mountain for that exciting-sounding event. Christmas lights glowed through the falling snow. Costumed singers serenaded us with familiar Christmas carols. Decorated wagons, four-wheelers, and buggies paraded down the street. A clown demonstrated magic tricks. A bank gave out Christmas ornaments. We tasted and gorged on meatballs, candies, cookies, cheese, hot chocolate, and roasted chestnuts offered by the various merchants. Christmas decorations intertwined with the stores' merchandise. A local rancher offered rides around town on a straw filled wagon that sported bells on the sides.

We saw friends from an area town in one of the stores. "We come every year," they told us. "Wouldn't want to miss it."

The event was so much fun. The next year we invited neighbors to attend with us. They were thrilled with the merchants' hospitality too. We sang carols with others in a music store. Tried out the various decorated cookies, chili-covered hot dogs, vegetables with dip, and cheese balls. We were intrigued with the various Christmas finery worn by the store workers — from Santa hats to colorful sweatshirts. There was a long line at the bakery for the hot Reuben sandwiches made while we waited. The unique mountain-style Christmas ornaments at one store caught our attention. We purchased a moose on snow skis to adorn our tree at home.

One year, as we headed back over the mountain to go home, we found the road closed due a heavy snowfall while we were enjoying the festivities.

Another road through the valley, seventy-five miles longer but at a lower elevation, was open. We arrived home safe, tired, and relieved to have avoided the closed road, but eager to go again another year.

We told friends, neighbors, and family about our fun time. It seemed to us that everyone would want to attend. "Don't eat supper before you go," we'd say. "There is plenty of food at this festive event. The merchants are eager for everyone to come." We attended for several more years, until we moved from the area.

Even though we miss attending this fun event, there is another supper we are invited to attend — the wedding supper of the Lamb. Revelation 19:9 (NLT) tells us, "Blessed are those who are invited to the wedding supper of the Lamb!... These are the true words of God."

God sends us the invitation, which is an honor. The Lamb is Jesus, who sacrificed his life to pay for the sins of mankind, so we could be forgiven. He is the Groom. Those who have believed in Jesus and accepted Him into our hearts and lives are called the Bride of Jesus Christ.

The supper will probably have some delightful surprises, as Larry and I experienced at the Christmas stroll. I wonder what kind of food will be served? Who will serve the food? Will there be special entertainment? How will God honor the Groom and bride? I'm hoping to see many people that I know.

However God has prepared this special occasion won't matter. It will be wonderful to be there. I'm looking forward to this grand event. God's works are magnificent, so we know this will be marvelous, too.

That will be a stroll to remember...forever.

~ Helen L. Hoover

29

My Red Balloon

Many of us may have forgotten treasures and remembrances of our life, lurking deep within the confines of a cardboard box, or as in my case, three boxes.

Dragging the boxes of pictures out from the back of the closet, I deliberately stacked them by the door of the guest bedroom, which also served as my office. I had moved those boxes too many times and I knew many of the pictures were of landscapes that weren't of any interest to me or anyone else. The pictures needed to be sorted and many of them thrown away, and I planned to digitize the ones I wanted to keep so my children would have some of my childhood pictures, as well as those of their ancestors.

The next morning it rained, a good excuse to rummage around in old boxes of pictures. As I anticipated, most depicted tranquil landscapes, aging barns or collapsing bridges; they made their way into the waste basket. I smiled at a picture of my dad as a child with his parents, standing by an old Model A Ford. That was a keeper!

I picked up an old snapshot that puzzled me. A red balloon was caught in the snare of some wet, bare, tree branches. Suddenly, the memory of a Christmas during my 30's came flooding into my mind, and I smiled, recalling God's care for me.

In retrospect, I know we won't always have a Norman Rockwell Christmas, yet, I discovered we can still worship Jesus the Christ, whose birthday we celebrate at Christmas.

While looking at the faded snapshot, a plethora of memories engulfed my mind. That had been a damp, bone-chilling Christmas Eve afternoon in Oakland, California. As manager of a temporary office agency, I had stayed long enough to fill orders for the day after Christmas.

After finishing, and being the only one left in the office, I turned off the lights and closed the office door. The click sounded loud in the empty building. I resolutely put a smile on my face, anticipating George down in the parking garage, asking me about my Christmas plans. Good-ol'-George was a protective grandpa to us single women who worked at the Broadway Office Building.

However, my smile turned to a frown as I realized what his reaction would be if he knew I was going home to an empty apartment on Christmas Eve. I had no plans for a date, let alone a party! That past year I had spent many lonely nights. I asked myself, "What difference does it make? It's just one more night." After entering the basement garage from the elevator, I quickly walked to my car. I saw George at one of the other automobiles, helping the owner get it started. "Merry Christmas, George," I shouted, in my cheeriest voice. "You, too, Miss Sam," he replied, lifting his head from inspecting the car motor under the front hood.

I was thankful to have avoided telling everyone of the lonely Christmas facing me. Easing the car out into the last minute rush of the Christmas Eve traffic, I noticed a soft drizzle had made the streets slippery, requiring all of my concentration as I drove the winding streets up into the hills above Oakland.

Normally, I enjoyed coming home to my second floor apartment. It was in an old, quaint European styled building which I loved. The one-bedroom apartment had a tiny dining room with French doors opening onto a little balcony seemingly floating in the tops of the trees. The living room had wide, dark wood framed windows with a view of the tree tops. A small fireplace sat at the side wall, perfectly cozy for the many chilly nights in the Bay Area.

I hung my damp coat in the closet, started a fire, and then put on some Christmas music.

I made a cup of my favorite cinnamon spice tea, and flopped into the spacious, cushioned chair by the fireplace, to contemplate what I was going to do with the rest of the Christmas weekend. Everyone I knew had either gone out of town to visit relatives or had made plans with friends. But not me this year. Self-pity was strange to me, but I decided I could indulge in it a little, after all, what difference did it make? There was no one to make miserable except me.

Over an hour passed as I dejectedly watched the rain, my mind twirling deeper and deeper into my self-made depression. Even in front of the blazing fire, my office clothes felt damp. A comfortable robe seemed in order. The bedroom was stuffy, so I opened the second floor window for fresh air.

Suddenly, I caught my breath. There, only a couple feet away, tenuously lodged in the wet, shiny, bare branches of the tree was a red balloon. I could not believe it. With breath-stopping clarity, I saw the rain drops on the tips of the branches, the wet balloon string waving in the breeze, even the balloon wobbling a little in its snare. It was there and it was for me!

I had no doubt in that instant, God Himself had sent me my little Christmas present, my red balloon. It might have seemed unimportant to anyone else, but the red balloon spoke to my hurting heart that He was aware of my loneliness, my frustrations, disappointments, betrayals and despair.

I chuckled as I watched my balloon float in the breeze, still snagged by the branches. I thought of rollicking children, the circus, country fairs, the many balloons I'd seen floating heavenward in parks and playgrounds. Elated, I snapped a picture of my red balloon.But most of all, I became aware of His love and care just when I needed Him most. It didn't matter that I was alone during the rest of the Christmas holiday. I had my red balloon out in the tree. And I was loved by my Father God, who understood my despair.

~ *Samantha Landy*

30

Waiting for the Surprise

Ihave always had a nosy streak in me. At times this can be good and at other times it can be to my detriment.

When I was seven years old, Christmas seemed to take eternity to arrive and the days slowly ticked by. I decided one day to go snooping and discovered my parents hiding spot. As I viewed all the beautiful toys hidden in their special hiding place, I oohed and aahed. I could not wait for Christmas day and play with those beautiful toys. After all, the doll I wanted, along with some much-needed clothes and a variety of other fun toys and treasures, were just awaiting my enjoyment.

I anxiously anticipated the arrival of Christmas day. The holiday drew closer. Ten days…nine…eight…five..three…two…one.

Finally, Christmas morning arrived. We celebrated at my grandparents' home, where we often spent Christmas in the early years of my childhood. I sprang from my bed and ran into the living room to see what was under the tree.

Sure enough, there was my Annie doll, Light Bright, stuffed animals and night gown that I'd found hidden.

I opened the presents with great delight, but was also bewildered to discover that part of the fun was taken out of opening my gifts. The more I dwelt on the reason, I realized it was because the surprise had been taken away.

This is a lesson that has stayed with me for decades.

Recently, Mama hinted at my upcoming Christmas present but I was content to wait and savor the surprise. On the other hand, I watch my brother, who takes great delight in sneaking an early peak at his gifts. In the last few years, it has become a game as I strive to find new and interesting ways to disguise his gifts and undermine his attempts for an early sneak.

Decades after I caught a sneak-peek of my Christmas gifts, I remember the lesson I learned. There are times when I wish I could gaze into the future and see what God has in the future for me. However, knowing in advance would take away all the surprise and awe God has in store.

Just as I no longer enjoy peeking in advance at my Christmas presents, I cannot peek into my future and all the wonders God holds for me there.

The best I can do is to seek God's will, decide my course of action, work hard and allow God to direct my steps. Proverb 3:6 (NLT) says, "Seek his will in all you do, and he will direct your paths."

Without fail, I know I will be surprised each and every time, because when I've allowed God to be in control, he has never done things the way I imagined. No, his ways are different, but his outcome is always much better.

I love waiting for God's surprises.

~ Diana Leagh Matthews

31

Our Beautiful Christmas Trees

"Come on, kids, lets get in the car and go cut our Christmas tree," Dad said. We hurriedly gathered our coats and scarves and climbed into the car. Our Christmas adventure was about to begin.

I was raised on the Monterey Peninsula in California which was surrounded by pine forests. The pines on the Peninsula were coastal pines with large, long needles. Many homes in my hometown of Pacific Grove were surrounded by these beautiful trees.

My father was employed by an oil company in Monterey and drove a big stove oil truck. He had many customers and over the years became good friends with his clients. One man, in particular, liked my dad and told him that he could bring his family and cut a Christmas tree on his property each Christmas. When Dad told my two brothers, sister and me, we were all excited at the prospect of cutting our own Christmas tree.

The time finally came and we were on our way to cut that special tree. Arriving at Dad's friend's home, he told us that he would have hot chocolate for us after we cut our tree. My two brothers set off into the woods. My dad, sister, and I began our hunt for our special tree. My brothers would show us their tree. My sister and I would show ours; of course, we always thought ours was the best. However, Dad would make the decision on which tree would be cut.

After cutting our tree and tying it to the roof of the car, we headed inside for the promised hot chocolate. Dad's friend was always gracious and happy that he provided a special gift of a tree to us.

While we were getting our tree, Mom was home rearranging furniture so our tree could be placed in front of the large picture window. She would clean the house and then get out the ornaments and tinsel.

Dad would put the tree in our tree stand and let us kids decorate it. After getting the ornaments on the tree, my brother placed each piece of tinsel on the branches. He was very particular, so that was a task left entirely to him.

Recently, I was looking at old photo albums of our family. I came across a picture of us gathered around our Christmas tree.

But wait! That couldn't be our tree. This poor tree was pitiful. The limbs sagged with ornaments hastily arranged and the tinsel was not put on as carefully as I remembered it.

As I gazed at the picture, I realized I had seen our Christmas trees with the eyes of a child, and there had been beauty in each of them.

Now, I see in the picture and the memory, that the beauty was in cutting the trees, the excitement of decorating them, and family time of sharing our stories.

The ultimate beauty of Christmas is in the reason for the celebration.

~ Beverly Hill McKinney

32

What Did You Get for Christmas?

For most, Christmas is a wonderful season.

I've lived in Edina, Minnesota; it was beautiful but brrrrr-cold! If you've ever called Minnesota home then you've probably celebrated Christmas surrounded by twenty-four-feet snow drifts and blistering winds of more than seventy miles per hour.

If you prefer to live in an area which many dream of, or at least dream of visiting, you might select Hawaii. I'm thinking it's at least seventy degrees warmer than the Midwest in December. If so you probably would have taken a photo of Santa surfing on Waikiki Beach in his colorful board shorts.

From Connecticut to California, Christmas is a wonderful holiday celebrating Christ's birth and expressing our love to those dearest to us.

Unfortunately, it is not a day of joy and fellowship day for all of us. In fact for some it is the worst day of the year as they find themselves eating a free supper from a local non-profit's soup kitchen. They stuff their cold, shivering hands into their penniless pockets, knowing they won't touch any coins, let alone dollar bills. Today they won't receive any gifts, cards and probably not even a handshake. They will feel all alone, isolated, insignificant, unwanted.

Saddest of all, they will feel unloved.

Although I had read stories of men and women who experienced the above, it had not happened to me, at least…not yet.

In 2010 I had to step aside from a promising career at a mega church in Palm Beach County. An interesting fact about this exquisite area of opulence is that it is the residence of over twenty-five billionaires and 71,221 millionaire households.

I received an alarming phone call from my stepfather that Mother was not doing well and I should return to the Asheville area of North Carolina, as soon as possible, and permanently!

What else could or should an only son do to show love to the person who brought him into this world? An even greater barometer is, what would Christ do?

I resigned and my wife and I gathered up our three small children and set sail for western North Carolina. Despite a track record of over fifteen years of ministry all over the country, I was not able to find a vacancy in a church in that area. I was eventually offered a position at a large Christian Conference Center where I would become their National Event Planning Manager, responsible for forty percent of the center's guest nights annually — which was 160,000 cumulative nights or $6.7 million in revenue.

Things did not go as desired. The Event Planning Departments was being relocated to their headquarters in the middle of the United States. Finding myself unemployed, I quickly looked for similar positions but none were available near Asheville, Greenville or Knoxville. I applied to area churches but there were no openings, or they felt someone from a mega church would never remain at a smaller church with limited resources.

After six months I landed a job with a non-profit organization at a significant drop in pay. That position lasted less than three months due to company layoffs. It was a time when our economy had faltered and scores of people were suffering; I was one of them. Despite working five part-time jobs I was not able to meet our basic expenses.

Life did not become more difficult, it became impossible. Not only financially but physically, socially, emotionally and even spiritually. I faced deep depression but had to plow on for the sake of my wife and children. One thing was consistent and that was my crying out to God day after day and hour after hour, "Where are you, God? Why? Why God? Please help me God."

One afternoon I ran into a businessman who owned a yogurt shop. He invited me to a Bible study attended by a group of local businessmen, held on Friday morning at an Atlanta Bread restaurant. I told him I would consider attending. But I doubted I ever would.

One day I awoke early and something kept telling me to attend that Bible study. During the study I was asked to share what I did and why I was there. The discussion leaders were a vice-president of a bank chain and a vice-president of Biltmore House, Biltmore Farms and its business complex, Biltmore Park.

During my story, a youth Pastor interrupted and said, "Guys, we've heard enough. We need to take up an offering and help this man now." Upon leaving, a man named John, head of Mission Hospitals Fund Raising Campaign said, "Tommy, please accept my gift and realize it's because God told me you need it. Don't say, 'No.'"

Later that day, Jack Brinkley, Director of Sports Outreach, called and said I was on his mind. Someone dropped off a coupon for a free Christmas tree from the Farmer's Market. He asked if Sandra and I would like one. We had told our daughters the night before we would probably not have Christmas and would also not have a tree this year.

Later, I was at my third part-time job at a local grocery store where I did a little bit of everything from cleaning restrooms, to stocking, cashier work and bagging groceries. One of my managers, making conversation, asked if I'd purchased all of my presents yet.

I paused then said "No," hoping that would end the conversation; but it did not. She continued, "Why not? It's almost Christmas Eve."

She kept looking at me. I finally blurted out, as my eyes swelled with tears, that I didn't have any money. "We are deep in debt, just had our car repossessed. I'm working five jobs but we still can't get a jump on our finances. I can't even afford a Christmas card for my wife." She told me to wait for a moment and she walked to her office. She returned and handed me an envelope full of cash, saying it was given to her by a customer who had owed her some money.

Later that night I told Sandra all that had happened that day and how God worked. We bowed and thanked God for being there for us. Later I stepped outside and looked up at a starry sky and told God I was sorry for doubting Him and He was truly the Creator of the Universe and capable of doing anything, at anytime, anywhere, for anyone.

The starlit sky was probably similar to what others looked at the night baby Jesus was born. It probably looked the same the night He died on the cross for my sins and the sins of the world. It will probably be the same sky that one day all who are believers will admire forever and ever.

You can be sure that God will take care of everything you need, his generosity exceeding even yours in the glory that pours from Jesus. (Philippians 4:19 MSG)

~ Tommy Scott Gilmore, III

33

Storefront Ministry

John opened a storefront mission on the streets of a large metropolitan city. He was just getting the mission started when a large gang moved into the area and began to threaten him. John asked for area churches to help run the storefront, feed the homeless kids who came in, and pray for the mission.

One night when John was running the storefront alone, a gang member named Rick wandered into the mission about midnight. Rick was high on amphetamines. His dark brown eyes looked wild. His normally golden brown skin was pale and lusterless. His breathing was shallow. John knew the boy was in danger from dying from an overdose, so he closed the storefront and hurriedly took the boy to an emergency room.

Rick stabilized after several hours. During Rick's recovery, John stayed at the hospital with him, leaving only to serve the storefront mission at night. Then, because Rick had no family or home other than the streets, John took Rick to his own home for a few days to recuperate.

After a few days at John's home, however, Rick disappeared into the anonymity of the streets. As days went by without hearing from Rick, John became depressed to think that Rick had returned to the gang.

Several weeks later, Rick again came to the mission near midnight. There were two boys with him, dressed in gang clothes. Both were struggling to breathe just like Rick had been several weeks earlier. John moved toward Rick to see if he, too was high on drugs. He appeared to be sober.

"These guys need help, John," Rick said. "I told them how you helped me."

John was taken aback because he assumed Rick had fallen into his old ways.

"I even told them about your Jesus. They probably don't believe it any more than I did. Maybe sometime they will."

John locked the door to the mission, helped the boys into his car, and once again headed to the emergency room. Over the next two years, the scene would be repeated over and over. Not all the boys got straightened out. Some of them died. In fact, John seldom saw or heard from the majority of them again. But Rick kept bringing them.

One night Rick joined John to speak at a fundraiser for the mission. When Rick told his story, John's missionary heart was full. It seemed worth all the sacrifice John had made for the mission just to see Rick's progress. Word was getting around the city about how to get out of the slavery of gangs and drugs.

John was on duty at the mission late Christmas Eve. Rick appeared at the door, holding a stumbling gang member. As John opened the door, a car slowed down nearby. Before John realized what was happening, a gun appeared through the open window of the car and a man shouted, "Merry Christmas Rick! Here's what we do to guys who take members from us!"

Shots rang out. Rick fell into John's arms, his eyes glazed with death. John's heart was breaking as he watched Rick's life ebbing. John stayed at the hospital and held Rick as he took his last earthly breath.

John was brokenhearted as he opened the door of the mission on the night after Rick's funeral. John asked himself over and over, "Where is God in all of this?"

John was angry as he looked at the Christmas tree in the window. It was now obscured from the outside by a piece of plywood replacing the windowpane that had been broken by a stray bullet. He hoped everyone would stay away that night. John thought about the gun that the police insisted he keep near the door in case trouble struck again. He saw the lights of a passing patrol car flash on the walls of the storefront.

Near midnight, the mission door slowly opened. Just as Rick had done so many times, one apparently sober boy dragged another boy high on drugs into the store. The sober boy said softly, "John, can you help my friend?"

Before John could answer the young man and welcome them to the mission, two police officers stationed nearby pushed their way into the storefront and grabbed both boys. One officer asked the boys what they were doing here. The sober boy shouted, "We came to see Rick's friend."

John stepped to the boys and asked the police officers to retire outside. "I can take care of this." They left reluctantly and stationed themselves right outside the door. John recognized one of the boys. He had been with Rick the night he was shot. He had been at Rick's funeral a few days later. Hope surged through John's depressed heart as he asked, "How can I help you?"

The boy hesitated.

"It's okay," John encouraged him.

"Rick told me about you. He said you were his friend. Can you help me and my friend, too? We want out."

As the years passed, many hundreds of teens passed through John's storefront mission. Many found their way out of drugs and gangs and a life of crime. Over the years, many gangs came and went through the city, but John was steadfastly available to help anyone who wanted out. A strange sense of respect grew up around the storefront ministry and never again did anyone come and threaten or harm John or those seeking help.

John retired last year and a young minister came to take over the mission. John took him aside and said, "This mission exists because of a brave boy named Rick. Let me tell you his story…."

The young man's face lit up with hope. The desire to minister exists because of the Jesus story.

~ Mary E. McQueen

34

Baloney Salad and Fruitcake

Please let it snow." I squashed my face against the front window and searched for a snowflake to fall from a gray Christmas Eve sky. Fog lay like a marshmallow blanket deep into the folds of the hollows and hid the mountains that surrounded our cozy Kentucky house.

"Karen, you're messing up my freshly cleaned windows. Get off—"

"Mama, do you think it's going to snow tonight?" I breathed onto the window and made it fog up even more. I moved over to a clear spot as a car slowed and turned into the driveway. "Mama, somebody just pulled into the driveway." I squealed in anticipation of a Christmas gift.

"Who is it?"

"I don't know. But they're in a cute little blue car."

"It must be Myrt and Bill. Hurry so we can get over to your granny's."

I wiped away the fog my breaths left on the window, leaving finger swipes in the wake. We put on our coats that Mama had been warming in front of the stove. Daddy loaded his arms with as much food and presents as he could hold. Mama and I grabbed the rest and we headed outside. Frigid air blasted us as we headed to Granny's house next door.

I sniffed the air down to my toes. "It smells like snow out here. Oh, it's just got to snow. It's Christmas."

We tromped onto Granny's porch and burst into the house. Mama put food on the dining room table as Daddy and I put gifts around Granny's aluminum tree. A rotating lamp with pie-shaped pieces of colored glass sat on the floor and turned the tree red, blue, gold and green.

We tossed our coats onto Granny's bed and then the hugging commenced. Aunt Myrt (short for Mary Ruth) told us stories about all the wonderful things she did this past year in Lexington. Myrt has a talent for tall tales.

The rest of the family started piling into the house with food and gifts. Aunt Joyce and her family, from Cincinnati, led the group in laughter.

Uncle Junior trapped me in a chair and came at me with his pinching fingers, like a crawdad, saying, "I'm gonna give you some sugar." I tried to escape, unsuccessfully, as he pinched my knees in just the right spot, making me wince in pain and scream for mercy. He always laughed like he thought I enjoyed the attack. I didn't.

I sat in the corner, mesmerized by the lamp as it reflected colors all over the room and made the tree and packages sparkle. I hoped the prettiest gifts had my name on the tags. Voices filled the house with boisterous laughter and teasing. Each time a new group of relatives arrived, the pile of presents grew until they created mounds of bright colors and reminded me of our mountains in the fall.

As the chill of the house became more obvious, we took turns standing in front of the fireplace to warm our fronts. Then, we turned around to warm our backs. We stood there long enough for heat to make our skin burn a little. That seemed to make the warmth last longer.

I breathed in the fragrance of burning wood mixed with fresh-cooked food now laid out on the dining table and buffet.

Granny appeared in the archway, wiped her hands on the skirt of her Christmas apron, and announced, "It's ready, everybody. Come and get it."

My stomach wanted some of everything. Instead, I chose foods I loved most — apple salad, Granny's sage dressing, buttered cornbread, shuck beans, pea salad, and my favorite — baloney salad sandwiches.

Every year, I watched Granny make the baloney salad the day of the party. She peeled the red wrapper off a huge log of baloney and cranked it through the metal meat grinder attached to her kitchen table. She added sweet pickles and boiled eggs to the mix. I loved watching the ingredients squish onto the metal plate, looking like baloney spaghetti. Then she added the mayonnaise and stirred it all in a huge pale green bowl. When it was just right, we spread the mixture onto white Bunny brand bread, sliced the sandwiches corner to corner and put them in the fridge to get cold. There's nothing as awesome as baloney salad sandwiches on Christmas Eve — except maybe my mom's fruitcake.

The men of the family always seemed to get to the head of the line. I silently prayed there'd be some food left by the time my turn came. We filled our plates and found an available seat from the menagerie of chairs and the sofa placed in a ring around the living room. Laughter and conversation dimmed as we scooped fork loads of fabulous mountain food into our mouths.

After we filled our stomachs to capacity, we opened presents. As Granny sat in her easy chair, aunts and uncles passed out the gifts. Granny always received more gifts than anybody else. All the grandkids had a gift from Granny, too. The grown-ups didn't get one. Aunt Mona Jo usually grabbed my gift from Granny and handed it to me so nobody could miss it.

"This one's for Kurn Lynn." (the hillbilly way of saying Karen Lynn) "Go ahead and open it!" She smiled as my face got hot. I tried to wait until everybody returned to their own presents, but she wouldn't let me off so easily. "Go on and open it. Let's see what it is."

I think Aunt Mona Jo knew what was in the box before I opened it. Actually, I knew what was in that box. I got the same thing from Granny every year — underwear. If I hesitated, Mona Jo helped me by ripping off the paper and opened the box for me.

I slunk down in my chair. I wanted to slide under the chair. Actually, I wanted to put Aunt Mona Jo under the chair as she said, "Oh, look at what Kurn Lynn got, everybody. Drawers. Ain't they purty? Hold 'em up so everybody can see how purty they are."

When the last gift had been opened and the room was littered with remnants of festive paper and bows, my aunts and Mom sneaked out of the room in whispers. They returned a moment later with the final gift for Granny — a Christmas stocking. It wasn't the normal red flannel stocking you might expect. It wasn't a knee sock like I hung from the window frame near the coal stove in my own house next door, either. They brought in a real nylon stocking, filled to the top with little gifts, fruit, nuts in the shells, and a variety of Christmas candies. It took the four of them to carry it into the room. Laughter erupted again. Granny's face turned all red like she was embarrassed. I know it embarrassed me since my uncles and boy cousins were in the room.

The party ended with a special treat Uncle Junior brought from Chicago — pink champagne. The kids weren't allowed to taste it. We sat and watched as the adults giggled when the bubbles tickled their noses.

Clean-up whizzed by as everybody stuffed the ripped paper and bows into trash bags. Then hugging commenced again. I liked that part. After the hugs ended, we filled our arms with gifts and a variety of leftovers to enjoy on Christmas day. Everybody said good-bye and Merry Christmas as my relatives packed their cars. Mama, Daddy, and I made our way across the yard toward our house. That's when I felt something cold hit my nose.

"Look! It's snowing. I knew it would snow. Woo-hoo! We're going to have a white Christmas." I danced across the yard, my head bent back to watch snowflakes fall from the sky.

Mama called to the relatives, "Y'all be careful driving back tonight. Them roads is gonna be slick."

Once inside, Mama sent me off to change into my PJs and then to warm myself in front of the stove before going to my unheated room. Stinging from the warmth of the coal stove, I ran and jumped into bed. Daddy pulled the heap of quilts over me to keep the warmth inside.

"Please read me a story, Daddy. The one about the baby Jesus being born."

He searched through the stack of books on top of the dresser he built for me when I was born. He sighed real big as he plopped on the edge of my bed to read. Even though it was one of my favorites, I felt my eyes start to sag before he got to the end. I yawned so wide my lips hurt.

"You'd better get to sleep now so Santa can come, Susie Q." That's what he called me when he was in a good mood. He gently kissed my forehead and ran his hard-working fingers across my hair.

"I will, Daddy. I sure hope it snows a lot so we can have snowcream for Christmas. Good-night." I yawned again and rubbed the hard knot of baloney salad sandwiches and fruitcake in my tummy. Thoughts of finding all the toys on my Christmas list under the tree in the morning, deep white snow covering the mountains, snowcream, and leftover baloney salad sandwiches chased each other in my head.

I wondered about the baby Jesus and what he got for his Christmas birthday. I hoped it wasn't underwear.

- Karen Lynn Nolan

35

I Am Bethlehem

We expect Christmas to be a joyous time. But for many, Christmas simply intensifies feelings of hopelessness and loneliness.

Many years ago, I struggled with depression as Christmas drew near. Wanting to keep my commitment as a choir member, I forced myself to participate in the Christmas concert. I broke down in tears before we entered the sanctuary. Friends, knowing my situation, hugged me. They gave me strength to compose myself and prepare to sing. As the concert proceeded, I began to listen with my heart to the words we sang:

> O little town of Bethlehem, how still we see thee lie.
> Above thy deep and dreamless sleep, the silent stars go by;
> yet in thy dark streets shineth, the everlasting light.
> The hopes and fears of all the years are met in thee tonight.

Dark streets. That sounds gloomy. That sounds like me.

As we went on to the second and third verses, I began to see what God was doing behind the scenes. "Where meek souls will receive Him still, the dear Christ enters in."

Suddenly, I sensed that God was speaking to me through the words of the song!

I am Bethlehem!

I thought of the verse in Galatians 4:4: But when the time had fully come, God sent forth his Son, born of woman, born under the law, to redeem those who were under the law, so that we might receive adoption as sons. And because you are sons, God has sent the Spirit of his Son into our hearts crying, "Abba! Father!" (Gal. 4:4-6 RSV).

Between songs, I quickly jotted down my thoughts on my bulletin. By the time the concert was over, I felt more hopeful and less lonely than I had in a long time. God's truth and presence were lighting up my darkness. This poem resulted from that experience:

I am Bethlehem...little, insignificant, inadequate in my eyes.
How long have I lain here still, hoping for a glimmer of Your glory,
going through the motions day after day?
LORD, You gave a promise through prophets long ago.
Will Your promise be fulfilled in me?
Will my purpose be fulfilled?
Above me, the stars are silent. My heart aches with their silence.
I anguish to hear Your voice.
But suddenly! Has the time fully come?
Here You are, shining in the dark streets of my heart, driving out gloom.
In Your radiance, You speak, giving Your Word flesh!
Therein my hopes are fulfilled, my fears dispelled.
O Glorious LORD! There is room in me for You!
Fill me to overflowing with Your glory!
Shine and speak through me.
Make Your music resound through me that others may know the song
You've given,
the peace You have brought.
Is this my purpose?...that You have come to be born in me?

This reminder by the Holy Spirit, that Jesus did indeed come to earth to be "born in me" (i.e. received by me as Savior and LORD) made my troubles fade into insignificance. Like Bethlehem of old, the only significance I need is to be a dwelling place of Christ. He is Emmanuel, God with us in all our problems. He gives us significance, adequacy, hope and comfort. He makes my heart want to sing with the joy of His presence.

- Judith Vander Wege

36

There's a Star in the East

I remember going to a Christmas Eve service when I was a small child. The traditional nativity pageant was acted out by nervous fourth-graders who wore bathrobes and had towels wrapped turban-like around their heads. Mary held a real wriggling four-month-old baby. I thought that Jesus was certainly alert and strong for a newborn baby. And big, too!

A large star, cut out of cardboard and covered with aluminum foil, shone over the manger. The pastor pointed to the star and said it was a sign in the eastern sky that Jesus was coming.

As we rode home that night, I asked Mama which direction was East. She pointed that out for me. Christmas morning, I was up before dawn, but didn't wake everyone to open presents. I had something else on my mind. I wanted to check out whether or not a star shone in the eastern sky.

I stole quietly outside and looked up in the direction Mama had shown me. Sure enough, one star was brighter than all the others. My heart began to pound. I could not wait to show it to Mama before the sun obscured it from view.

I scurried into the house shouting, "There's a star in the East! There's a star in the East!"

Needless to say, the rest of the family were not thrilled about going out to see the star. But finally, Mama and my sister dragged themselves from bed and went out with me to look. The star was fading fast as the first rays of sunshine stole across the Christmas morning sky, but still beautifully visible.

Years later, when I was a parent of five children, Christmas came around and I remembered that morning long ago. I woke early and looked out. Sure enough, there was one star brighter than all the others in the early morning sky.

My husband smiled sleepily and said, "Mars, probably."

That didn't matter. I picked up the phone at 6 A.M., 4 A.M. on the west coast where Mama lived, and dialed Mama's number.

"There's a star in the East!" I shouted when she answered the phone. "Look, there's a star in the East!"

"You nut." She laughed. But she looked out her window then said, "I can't see it from here, Mary."

"I know," I told her, "because you can only see it in your heart. Merry Christmas, Mama."

"Merry Christmas, Baby," she said, "and... thanks for remembering."

Over the years, we often began our Christmas greetings to one another with, "Look, there's a star in the East!"

Sometimes Mama was at our home visiting and sometimes, like that first Christmas I called her, she was in her home in San Diego. Last year, Mama had gone home to heaven. But I went outside on Christmas morning and looked up. I said to the sky, "Look, there's a star in the East."

And somewhere from on high, I heard the sound of my mama's laughter once again. "You nut." Her voice whispered into my heart. "Thanks, Baby, for remembering."

Over 2,000 years ago a baby's first cries announced that the world had changed. The Bible tells us the skies were filled with light from a star in the east and the sounds of angelic voices singing in a mighty chorus, "Glory to God in the highest. And to all on earth, peace."

May your heart be filled as you make wonderful memories of times spent with ones you love this Christmas season. Why not get up a little early on Christmas morning and check out the eastern sky. The star will be there, still lighting the skies with a message of hope. For you see, it's still true. "There's a star in the East! There's a star in the East!"

~ *Mary E. McQueen*

Christmas Azalea

Be ready in season and out of season.

2 Timothy 4:2 NKJV

On a dreary day during the first week of December, I was busy putting the finishing touches on my Christmas decorations. I stepped onto the front porch in the icy chill to adjust my wreath and saw something shocking.

My largest azalea bush sported a single red flower. I blinked my eyes a few times, thinking I was mistaken. Surely, something red was caught on one of the branches. Moving closer to inspect the bush, my mind quickly calculated the months until blooming season — three to four months away. There was no way this fragile plant would be putting out a blossom in December. But sure enough, there it was in all its glory. One magnificent bloom. Out of season. The sight of something so beautiful and unexpected brightened my day and made me smile.

The Bible tells us to be ready in season and out of season. This scripture makes me wonder how ready I am to follow God's leading and be a blessing to others, in season and out. When it's convenient and when it's not. Whether I'm prepared or whether I'm not. And when I'm expecting it or when I'm not.

Another Scripture (Proverb 25:11 ESV) says a word fitly spoken is like apples of gold in settings of silver. According to Dictionary.com, the word *fitly* means "in a proper or suitable manner, at a proper or suitable time." We could say, whatever is appropriate and fitting for the occasion. What a perfect picture of something spoken to the right person, at just the right time, and in the right circumstance.

In other words, whenever the opportunity presents itself, in season and out.

The holidays provide the best opportunity to practice this gift of blessing others with our time, our love, and our words. Hearts are open and more ready to receive than at any other time of the year. Let's be like my Christmas azalea and proudly let the light of Jesus shine through us as never before.

His love is never out of season.

~ Andrea Merrell

It Took a Miracle

Christmas the year I was eleven stands out from all the others I've known. Daddy drove Mother, my brother Jimmy and me from our home in Dothan, Alabama to Charlotte, North Carolina. We had spent past Christmases with Grandmother and Granddaddy Wilson, but never like this one.

We arrived at 800 Hillside Avenue but Grandmother didn't come outside to meet us. Granddaddy slowly descended the porch steps with his head bent. I ran to hug him and he squeezed me extra tightly. As I looked up into his blue eyes, the twinkle was missing. He hugged Mother and Jimmy but when he hugged Daddy I noticed his shoulders shaking as he said, "Son, I'm so glad you all got here in time."

The small kitchen had not changed since my earliest memory except Grandmother wasn't there. Cousins, aunts and uncles crowded together. After we hugged and greeted each other I walked on through the den past the big desk where Grandmother did the accounting for Granddaddy's plumbing business. I saw the old upright piano where I had enjoyed playing the old hymns many times. Although more people than usual were in the house, it seemed still and lonely.

I didn't care what the house looked like or that there were no welcoming smells coming from the kitchen. I didn't care that there wasn't a Christmas tree in the living room. Only one thing was on my mind: seeing my beloved grandmother. When I went through the darkened hall and stood outside her bedroom door, my aunt said, "No honey, don't open it. Just stay out here. Grandmother's resting."

By then, Mother and Daddy had joined me. Daddy opened the door and eased into the room. A little while later he motioned for Mother to go in with him. The door closed again. I waited. Finally they came out into the hall. Their faces were wet with tears. I said, "Please let me go in. I want to see Grandmother."

They looked at me and then looked at each other. Mother said, "She doesn't look like you remember her. She's very sick." I knew she had been sick, but she was still my grandmother.

Daddy said I could go in and stand by the far side of her bed and speak to her, but that she might not recognize me or be able to speak. It was night outside but nothing was as dark as that room when I tiptoed in, where I had spent many nights, sleeping on a cot at the foot of my grandparents' bed.

That wasn't my grandmother! Somebody was playing a terrible trick on me. She had always been robust and full of laughter and life. This person looked like a bag of bones covered with mustard-colored skin. I bent closer and realized that this really was Grandmother Wilson. I prayed that the Lord would help me as I reached for her hand. "Grandmother, it's Sally. If you know who I am, please squeeze my hand."

I waited. It seemed she didn't know me.

Wait...

Was that a squeeze?

Yes! She squeezed my hand again. I began to tell her that I loved her and I had been praying for her and would see her in heaven if she didn't get well.

Mother opened the door and motioned for me to come out so others in the family could see Grandmother one last time. I had never experienced such feelings before. I had never watched any of my loved ones die. I found a quiet corner where I could be alone with my thoughts and pour out my sorrow to the Lord. I was young and a young Christian so there was much I didn't understand.

I began to listen to the older family members as they worried aloud that Uncle Charles might not make it in time. They had called several times and begged him to come if he wanted to see his mother again. Still he hadn't come. I began to understand that he was the "black sheep" of the family. He had not accepted Jesus into his heart and life. That was heavy on the hearts of Grandmother and Granddaddy who had prayed for him many years.

That night Grandmother went into a coma and the end seemed to be near. Everyone tiptoed around and whispered, very unnatural for our usually loud, fun loving family. Suddenly the phone rang and the volume increased. Uncle Charles said he was on his way from Louisiana. Everybody was mad because he had waited until it was convenient for him.

A couple days passed with no change. The doctor said she could linger or she might die at any time. One day the door opened and in walked Uncle Charles. His brothers and sister told him that he should have come sooner, that she couldn't communicate. But he insisted on going in to see her.

He said, "Mother, it's Charles. I'm here. I love you."

She hadn't spoken since the night we got there. But suddenly Grandmother Wilson opened her eyes and said, "Oh, Son. I've been waiting for you to come. I wanted to ask you one more time to ask Jesus to come into your heart and save you from your sins. I want to be sure that you will meet me in heaven."

That big, strong, crop-duster pilot began to sob and say, "Yes, Mother. I will. I'll give my life to Jesus and I promise you, I'll meet you in heaven."

There was much rejoicing because now the family circle was complete. We were all Christians. The next day Grandmother slipped back into a coma and finally breathed her last breath on earth.

We were sad but so glad that God honored her years of praying and let her see her wayward son come home to Jesus.

That was December 23rd. Her funeral was on Christmas Eve. I remember only one song sung at her service. That was, "It Took a Miracle."

It really did. The Christ of Christmas gave our family the best gifts possible; my uncle's salvation and healing Grandmother by taking her to heaven to spend her first Christmas with Jesus where she is no longer suffering.

~ Sally Wilson Pereira

39

Unforgettable Christmas Gifts

I once received an email captioned "The First King Size Bed." It showed a crude wooden manger, the best Mary and Joseph could give their newborn son.

The illustration triggered memories gleaned from seven-plus decades of Christmases. Of giving and receiving gifts, many now forgotten, others indelibly impressed on my heart and mind for a variety of reasons.

I was born during the Great Depression. Presents were as humble as that straw-filled feedbox, often acquired at great sacrifice and anticipated by starting preparations in January for the following Christmas. Mom and my aunts spent hours embroidering pillowcases and dish towels and making potholders for the women, scraping together bits of money to buy remembrances for the men and children. I still remember Mom "making a list and checking it twice" (or more) to make sure no one was forgotten.

My brothers and I had been taught that it's the thought that counts, not the gift. "You don't have to say you like something," our parents said. "Just be gracious and say 'thank you.'"

One Christmas, Dad had the opportunity to role-model this teaching. He opened his present from a beloved aunt who had a talent for giving outlandish gifts. He held up a soap-on-a-rope, designed for use in a shower. This was before our old-fashioned house had running water. We had no shower. I don't know how Dad kept a straight face when with his usual Southern courtesy, he thanked my aunt for the inappropriate gift.

When I was ten or eleven I washed windows and cupboards to earn money for my first 'store-boughten' presents. I felt richer than Rockefeller walking the aisles of the five-and-dime store armed with my four, hard-earned quarters. After only two hours of shopping, I was the proud possessor of a tiny Christmas corsage for Mom, a bandana for Dad, and a gift I don't remember for my older brother. Best of all, a charming monkey bank for my little brother. Randy's joy as he saw the jaunty little guy tip his hat when someone dropped in a penny erased the memory of my wrinkled fingers and aching muscles from scrubbing.

Years passed. After World War II ended, money was a little more plentiful. One Christmas, Mom and Dad gave me two short-sleeved pullover sweaters from JC Penney's, one turquoise blue and the other American beauty rose. (I think they cost $3.99 each.)

One unforgettable Christmas, Mom surprised Dad with twenty Zane Grey novels at sixty-nine cents each. That luxury brought the family hours of reading on snowy evenings around the large wood-burning heater. The books instilled in us a love for western history. We read them so many times we knew the characters and plots by heart, as well as the settings.

Years later, Dad took us on camping trips throughout the western states. We often recognized places from the books, such as where a certain cowboy watered his horse. In Oak Creek Canyon on the way to Sedona, Dad pointed and said, "There's the inn where Carly in *The Call of the Canyon* stayed." A sign confirmed it. The long-range effect of that Christmas gift is staggering. Dozens of my inspirational novels have their roots in those books and the places we later visited.

Another never-to-be forgotten gift came long after Mom had stopped making quilts for our family. Dad once more lowered the quilting frame he had built and attached to our high dining room ceiling. Mom painstakingly began making gorgeous quilts for my two brothers' wives. Her labor of love brought a lump to my throat and mist to my sisters-in-law's eyes.

Not all the gifts were tangible. I will never forget an unusual gift from Dad and my younger brother. Mom was teaching in our small school. I was the school secretary. One particular year, school wasn't being dismissed until noon on Christmas Eve Day. My older brother and his large family were due to arrive that afternoon and stay through the New Year. The extended family would be there that night for supper and our gift exchange. Then again on Christmas Day for a big dinner.

On the 23rd, I was feeling depressed. My "still-must-do" list, including decorating the huge fir tree shedding snow on the back porch, haunted me.

How could we get everything done by the next night?

I picked Mom up after school and slowly drove home, careful not to let her know all I wanted to do was drop everything else, and get a good night's sleep. When I trudged in the front door my gaze went through to the dining room. The tip of a beautiful star-topped fir tree touched our ten-foot ceiling. Tinsel, icicles, and Christmas balls reflected the warm glow of red, green, and blue Christmas bulbs on the perfectly decorated tree. Randy had come home from college and he and Dad had created this vision of beauty.

I cried.

My immediate family members are all gone now. I celebrate Christmas with Randy's children and grandchildren. We give and receive gifts according to our circumstances. Yet I will never forget Christmases past. There, my brothers and I learned the true meaning of giving, represented by sacrifice, a monkey bank, unexpected sweaters, Zane Grey books, hand-made quilts, a gracious response to soap-on-a-rope, and a beautifully decorated tree.

But above all, I learned the true meaning of Christmas from a humble, straw-filled manger that housed the greatest gift ever given.

- Colleen L. Reece

40

The Greatest Christmas Present

Some people have said my life has been a testimony of close calls, pain, prayer and hope. Like stones dropped in a pool, these difficult and often dangerous experiences have had radiating significance for me and many others. Yet it often takes the dark to make the light stand out. If there were only bright pieces in our quilts of life, God knows we wouldn't fully appreciate them.

For example, in Montana in 1963, I was on a train bound for Anchorage, Alaska to join my soldier-husband at Fort Richardson. There had been extensive flooding in this area of Montana due to an early spring mountain thaw. Some of the railroad tracks had been washed out, so our train was rerouted onto an old rail line. Mere moments after the last car passed over a trestle above a river in a deep canyon, the trestle we'd just crossed collapsed into the gorge.

Then, on Good Friday of 1964, my husband, Roland, and I survived a devastating earthquake in Anchorage. In March of 1987, Roland was diagnosed with a malignant kidney tumor. Due to a combination of the tumor and a separate kidney disease, he no longer had functioning kidneys and had to undergo dialysis three times a week for the rest of his life.

John, our eighteen-year-old son, was diagnosed with an incurable kidney disease in 1989. On January 6, 1992, one of my young nephews was accidentally shot and killed. A few months later, my father was diagnosed with a rare form of lymphoma brain cancer. These challenging circumstances were not the end of a long list.

My most dramatic personal experience occurred on December 24, 1983. It was 4 A.M. and outside our country home two miles south and two miles west of Palmyra, a town with a population of about five hundred, approximately twenty miles southeast of the capitol city of Lincoln, Nebraska, the wind was a mini-gale and snow was falling as thick as a multitude of burst-open feather pillows in front of a thousand giant fans.

As office manager for the 56th Street and Highway 2 Dallman's IGA store n Lincoln, I was a compulsive worker. I was always on the job and never ick. Normally, I didn't have to be at work until 6 A.M., but the day before ve had been having computer problems and my boss wanted me there early on Saturday to help resolve them. I'd made the twenty-mile drive to work hrough many previous difficult winters and didn't intend to let a little snow and cold stop me this time.

When I left for work, I had no idea of how treacherous and severe weather conditions had become between our home and Lincoln. But I'd made the drive hundreds of times before in bad weather and never gave it much thought. Conditions began to deteriorate rapidly as soon as I pulled out of our driveway. It wasn't long before I began experiencing the most intense physical and emotional misery I'd ever encountered in my thirty-nine years on Earth.

It was a little over two miles north from our home to Highway 2, the main route from Palmyra into Lincoln. As I drove through the intersection marking the first mile, large snowdrifts began appearing before me. Not far from the main road, my initial unsettling, stomach-grabbing moment occurred. My car suddenly high-centered on a drift. The wheels spun crazily. There was no traction. That's when I first glanced at the gas gauge. It registered a quarter of a tank.

I mentally estimated how long that much gas would last. Hopefully, it would be enough until snowplows arrived to clear the road. I knew I'd never be able to walk two miles back home, because of the icebox cold air. And this dirt road wasn't well-traveled, especially at 4:30 A.M. on a Saturday that happened to be Christmas Eve morning.

Snow was blowing so hard I couldn't get my bearings to determine exactly where I was. Periodically, a car's headlights would appear on Highway 2. That's when I'd begin flashing my headlights in an attempt to catch the driver's attention. I'd start the car for a few minutes and then switch it off. The possibility of carbon monoxide poisoning scared me, so I rolled down my window a little to compensate. Of course, this made it even colder.

It seemed forever before headlights again appeared on Highway 2. Two beams of light moved slowly west toward Lincoln. I again flashed my lights on and off. Miraculously, this car turned off Highway 2 onto my road, stopped and began flashing its lights. We continued this silent communication back and forth for a little while.

I was aware it wouldn't be wise to leave my car under these conditions, but it appeared this person was waiting for me. The other car didn't appear to be that far away. I turned off my lights and got out, figuring this person would realize I was on my way on foot.

I wasn't wearing boots, just regular shoes. I had on long woolen socks and stretch slacks, a sweater, a winter coat, a neck scarf wrapped around my head and tied around my neck, my son's gloves, plus an afghan from the car that I put over my head to protect me from the freezing wind. It was now approximately 5 A.M.

It wasn't long before I lost the afghan in the wind and multitude of snowdrifts, most of which extended above my knees. My scarf soon disappeared, too. The wind and snow slapped against my face making it burn like tiny pinpricks. I could hardly maintain an upright position in the wind and had to hunch over to make any headway. The swirling snow forced me to close my eyes. I kept zigzagging back and forth across the road. Every now and then I glanced up to focus on the headlights in order to get my bearings.

I fell into the drifts again and again. Before long, my legs became numb. I couldn't feel them anymore. Then I collapsed onto one drift and it felt warm. I was physically exhausted and only wanted to sleep. I had no desire to get up.

A disturbing thought entered my mind at that moment. If I died, my three kids might overlook the significance of Christmas as Christ's birthday and only associate it with their mother's death. That's when I prayed and asked God to help and give me the strength to get up again. I attempted to move, but my legs had no feeling. I had to grope for them in the dark and snow and manually position them under me for balance. Somehow, I got up and began stumbling toward the headlights once more.

But this car now appeared to be backing up in the darkness. If it left, I knew I'd be left alone in the middle of nowhere to die. I panicked and began yelling.

"Hey, I'm here! Help me! Don't leave me!"

I stopped shouting and began to pray again. A few moments later, I heard a man yelling back at me. Although he couldn't see me, he'd waited until I was about halfway before he got out of his car. He knew he couldn't make it all the way to my car and back to his in the severe cold without additional protection. His car hadn't been backing up. It was merely an optical illusion created by the wind, snow and my exhausted condition.

"Who are you?" were his first words. It was Ken Sturdy. He was a correctional sergeant at the Nebraska State Prison in Lincoln and had been on his way to work when he saw my flashing lights and knew someone was in trouble. I'd known him and his family since he was twelve. He hadn't recognized me because of the huge patches of frostbite on both of my cheeks and a left ear that was swollen two to three times its normal size. I was also covered with snow.

Ken grabbed my arm and began pulling me toward his car. I kept stumbling because of the deep drifts and not being able to feel my legs.

"Go on without me," I cried, after another demoralizing fall. "Leave me here and go get help. I can't make it!"

"You *will* make it!" Ken yelled back at me above the wind. "Come on, the car's close and it's warm." He was well aware that I'd die if he left me.

We finally reached the safety of his car which he'd kept running. As I collapsed on the front seat, the first thing I heard was a weather report on his radio stating that the wind chill, fueled by 40 mph winds, had plunged to 77 degrees below zero. I was exposed to this inhospitable temperature for approximately thirty minutes in what was later discovered to be a trek of nearly half a mile.

Ken drove me to his home in Palmyra. With his wife Marlene's assistance, they began to thaw me out. I had uncontrollable shivering fits for hours.

During that half-hour of life-threatening exposure, my chin froze to my neck. The skin is still leathery there, even all these years later. One ear was swollen beyond belief. My watch froze to my arm. Both of my legs discolored and scabbed over from frostbite. They still carry these scars. And a gap between my coat and gloves added two more bands of frostbite.

The roads weren't cleared until about 5 P.M. That's when my husband and a friend were finally able to reach me in a four-wheeled vehicle. When I got home that evening, I called one of my best friends, Judy Meyer, in Lincoln.

"Guess what, Judy? "I said. "You won't believe what I got for Christmas. It's the greatest present anyone could ever get."

"What is it?" Judy asked excitedly.

"Life," I replied.

I'd been taught from my earliest days in Sunday school that God is in control of everything. And I believe He sent Ken to help save my life that Saturday morning in 1983. God heard my prayers and answered them.

People often ask what I've learned through this experience and all of those other difficulties. I tell them that I now count my blessings, not my problems, each day. I don't know why things have turned out this way, but I believe God has a purpose for everything that's happened and someday I'll know the reasons why they occurred. In the meantime, I continue to maintain my faith, knowing that hardships are a part of this life and that God's love and power will continue to sustain and give me the courage to go on. But the main thing these experiences have taught me is that God is always available to help His children rise above their circumstances.

- Rosemary Luebke
as told to Robert B. Robeson

41

A Gift for God This Christmas

The book, *Who is Coming to Our House?* by Joseph Slate, is a story told from the animals' perspective as they busily prepare for the arrival of Baby Jesus. Each animal describes his/her contribution in preparing the house — their barn.

- Ram dusts.
- Chick sweeps.
- Goose stacks the hay and uses her feathers to make a soft bed.
- Horse nudges the door ajar.
- Hen lays an egg.
- Spider uses her talent to spin a new web.
- Peacock displays his feathers.
- Owl uses his time to watch for their guest — the Savior.
- Cat and rat, however, are doubters who complain.

Mary and Joseph appear, weary from travel, and all the animals say, "Welcome, welcome, to our house!" The animals are excited to warmly embrace the Baby Jesus.

To show their enthusiasm, they gave all they could give to welcome Him.

God also gave us all He could give. He gave us His son, Jesus. His gift was a pure gift of love. Because we love Him, we may wish we could give God a gift in return.

The animals in this simple story speak a profound truth. They show us what we can give to Jesus. We can give Him our:

- Work
- Talents
- Time
- Heart
- Trust
* Excellence
- Service
- Glory

Work

Colossians 3:23 NIV tells us: Whatever you do, work at it with all your heart, as working for the Lord, not for human masters.

Whether our work is inside the home or outside it, what we do can become an act of worship. While working we can praise Him for the house we sweep, the tools to perform our duties, and the health to accomplish them.

Talents

Have you ever watched a spider weave a delicate web? It is amazing to say the least. God equipped the spider with that unusual ability because He knew the spider would need it.

When God designed you, He embedded within you particular passions, abilities, and talents. These attributes enable you to fulfill your purpose, advance God's kingdom, bring glory and attention to God, and serve others.

Hebrews 13:20-21 NASB tells us: Now the God of peace, who brought up from the dead the great Shepherd of the sheep through the blood of the eternal covenant, even Jesus our Lord, equip you in every good thing to do His will, working in us that which is pleasing in His sight, through Jesus Christ, to whom be the glory forever and ever. Amen.

God has equipped you with the tools to share your gifts. Tools can be your personal attributes, your passions, and even the people He places in your life. What tools do you think God has given you?

Time

The wise owl used his time looking for the guest — the Savior. It is important that we, too, look for the Savior — in our everyday circumstances and in anticipation of Christ's return.

Ephesians 5:15-17 ESV tells us: Look carefully then how you walk, not as unwise but as wise, making the best use of the time, because the days are evil. Therefore do not be foolish, but understand what the will of the Lord is.

The owl is known for its wisdom. But James 1:5 NIV tells us: If any of you lacks wisdom, you should ask God, who gives generously to all without finding fault, and it will be given to you.

We can ask God to help us know how to best manage time and to show us how to spend our time on His will and not waste it on things that do not matter.

Psalm 90:12 NASB tells us: So teach us to number our days, that we may present ⊃ You a heart of wisdom.

Life is short — and death is certain.

Heart

The horse nudged the door open. He's ready. Excited. Anticipating Jesus!

We too can nudge open our heart to God.

Matthew 22:37 NIV tells us: Love the Lord your God with all your heart and with all your soul and with all your mind.

The heart represents our desires and affections. It is who we are; it's our mind, emotions, and our will. God wants us!

Trust

The cat and rat were both doubters. They refused to believe that a guest would come. They, therefore, also rejected the invitation to prepare. They didn't believe or trust what they were hearing.

Often we doubt God's presence and trust His plan for our life, especially when times are tough.

Cast out doubt and believe that God is coming to your house to care for you. Choose to believe that God is good, works everything together for our good, and is faithful to keep His word.

Proverbs 3:5-6 ESV tells us: Trust in the Lord with all your heart, and do not lean on your own understanding. In all your ways acknowledge Him, and He will make straight your paths.

Trust that God knows the best route for you. Trust that He has a plan.

Excellence

Resist mediocrity. Mediocrity is average, ordinary, and commonplace — getting by with the very least. The Hen gave an egg. It was all she had to give. But it was also her very best.

Let's follow her lead and be excellent in our work. Refuse the temptation to compare what we give as unworthy, or to think that another's gift is better.

Proverb 13:4 ESV tells us: The soul of the sluggard craves and gets nothing, while the soul of the diligent is richly supplied.)

The person who cleans up another's mess and the person writing report in the office might appear to only being doing their jobs. But when they do quality work to the best of their ability, they are glorifying God with excellence

Service

All the faithful animals (not the doubters) served together for the common good.

First Corinthians 12:7 tells us: A spiritual gift is given to each of us so we can help each other.

What a relief to know that our service isn't dependent on our skills alone. God uses willing hearts and empowers us to serve others.

Glory

The peacock presented his beautiful colors in anticipation of the arrival of King Jesus. He spread his beauty to glorify Him.

In Jeremiah 9:23-24 NKJV, the Lord tells us: Let not the wise man glory in his wisdom, let not the mighty man glory in his might, nor let the rich man glory in his riches; but let him who glories glory in this, that he understands and knows Me, that I am the Lord, exercising lovingkindness, judgment, and righteousness in the earth. For in these I delight, says the Lord.

We glorify God when we give Him the credit.

We glorify God when what we do points others to Jesus.

We glorify God when we praise Him for our abilities.

We glorify God when we thank Him.

Matthew 5:16 NASB tells us: Let your light shine before men in such a way that they may see your good works, and glorify your Father who is in heaven.

We can give these eight gifts to God. And with joyful response we will say, *Welcome, welcome, to our house!*

– Deborah M. Presnell

42

Christmas Presence

We've scheduled your husband's heart procedure for tomorrow. As soon as we complete his discharge papers, the ambulance will take him to Louisville. If all goes as planned, he should be transferred to the rehabilitation hospital the following day."

Although Christmas was only four days away, I embraced that incredible news. Our family had gone from the doctor saying, "We can't ever say there's no hope, but it doesn't look good," on December 10, 2009, to witnessing unbelievable recovery in the days that followed.

A heart attack, stroke, fall resulting in a severe brain injury, and lack of oxygen from an extended period with no heart or lung function, plus a 2004 diagnosis of a malignant brain tumor — any one can result in death. All together, death is almost guaranteed. Almost.

A surgeon friend, in the same Sunday school class as my husband, was on duty when my husband entered the emergency room. He volunteered to meet with the family. Not one to hold back bad news, he shared the numbers indicating almost no brain activity. We could remove the respirator immediately or wait. He anticipated no difference in the ultimate results.

My husband had said for years he never wanted his death prolonged by artificial means and had signed a medical directive to that effect. However, we chose to wait until we saw a cardiologist.

This decision followed group prayer with two of our pastors, two family members, and two close friends. As each person prayed, God's love and our love for one another filled the room. With tears streaming, I thanked God for time with my husband, prayed for healing, and expressed thanks for whatever the future held. I acknowledged the superiority of God's love over my own and placed my trust in that love.

Friends from church and community came and went, praying, hugging, and loving. Family members arrived for what we thought were final goodbyes. One at a time, they held my husband's hand, talked to him, and shared their love.

When staff moved him from the emergency room, the waiting area quickly filled. My sister remained in the room with me through the night. I held my husband's hand and prayed, not so much with words as with my heart.

Around 3 A.M. the reality that he might die in a few hours hit full force. I lowered my head against the bed rail and quietly sobbed. Within minutes, God flooded my soul with His presence. I learned later that a friend awoke around 3 A.M., so burdened she couldn't sleep. Although she prayed for my husband, she focused on my need for comfort and strength.

Near dawn, my husband's arm moved around my waist. Although he had exhibited involuntary movement earlier, this felt different. It felt deliberate. And I thanked God for that moment.

Later in the day, when staff removed his ventilator, my husband breathed on his own, tracked motion and sound with his eyes, and responded with hand squeezes to questions. Within another twenty-four hours he was sitting up, talking, and soon making jokes.

The surgeon, who uses such language sparingly, stated openly, "Well, it looks like we have us a miracle."

The cardiologist, who didn't see us again until the following week, charted the little known medical word, "Wow!"

My husband's new nickname, The Miracle Man, spread throughout the hospital, our church, and the community.

The day EMS loaded him for the hospital transfer, I made a beeline home to pack our essentials for the next few weeks. After gathering clothing, personal items, and reading and writing supplies, I realized we had to celebrate Christmas too. So I grabbed a small crocheted Christmas tree and a miniature nativity scene. Satisfied the two were perfect for the days ahead, I added what Christmas gifts I'd purchased before all our excitement. Then I said goodbye to our house with its far more elaborate decorations.

The next day's news could not have been better. I nodded as the doctors talked and pointed. A short time later we prepared for our final transfer.

Most that I packed from home remained in the car until my husband was successfully settled in the rehabilitation hospital the next afternoon. Since they had extra bed space during the holidays, they approved my request to move into the room with him. I was firmly convinced this was vital for my husband's mental, physical, and emotional recovery, plus my own sense of well-being. I told them, "He's lost both long- and short-term memory, and I'm his memory bank. I need to be there to help him review the past and verify the accuracy of any recall."

In addition, his weak muscles and poor balance placed him at increased risk for another fall. In spite of a bed alarm, he could hit the floor before staff reached him. I never had to present that argument. It spoke for itself immediately after our arrival. When a worker escorted me to his room, he wasn't there. While she asked other staff, "Where's Mr. Derringer?" I checked the bathroom door. Left briefly unattended, he somehow made it to the bathroom alone, a terrifying way to begin his stay.

Above all, I believed in the healing power of love. He needed to know that he wasn't in this battle alone. I wanted to offer as much normalcy as possible ...to touch him and tell him "I love you" several times a day...to eat and sleep with him...to talk, read, and watch TV together...and to pester the daylights out of him when he grew weary of all the hard work ahead.

So we began our daily routine of physical, occupational, and speech therapy. I reinforced the staff's efforts, using their suggestions. When I included additional ideas from our seasoned speech therapist sister-in-law, the young hospital therapist applauded our efforts and added them to her bag of tricks. The hospital schedule proved extremely taxing for both of us, but we knew immediate, intensive therapy resulted in faster and more successful recovery.

During free time, my husband often slept. His body needed that extra rest for maximum healing. We looked at family pictures and tried to remember names. We talked about the recent and not so recent past and how everyone fit into it. We discussed his employment history. We relived our favorite vacations. We brought the past into the present — over and over again.

Although separated by several miles, friends and relatives continued to make brief, well-spaced visits. A few joined us on Christmas Eve and Christmas day. Siblings helped fill in the gaps of gifts not yet purchased and made desired deliveries for us.

But we also had several hours alone. During that time, I gazed at our tiny tree and nativity scene. In spite of the challenges we'd faced and those that lay ahead, my heart overflowed with the blessings we'd received. In a half joking, half serious way, I told a few late visitors, "I've learned that all a person really needs is enough to eat, a warm place to sleep, and someone to love."

Our solitude provided time to contemplate anew the significance of Christmas and the gift of love and life offered to our world. I gained a greater appreciation for Mary and Joseph's predicament that first Christmas night as well. Far from home, they faced their medical dilemma and unknown future alone in a shelter intended for livestock. Sure, they had visitors after Jesus' birth, but those men were strangers, not the people they knew and loved. I could not imagine how intimidated they must have felt with the unparalleled task that lay before them and their newborn son.

So I gave thanks. Thanks that we were together. Thanks that we had abundant medical and emotional support. Thanks for a warm, comfortable place to stay until we could return home. Greater still, thanks that, because of God's Presence to earth that night so long ago, we would never have to face the future alone.

Ever Present God
There are times in our lives when
the pain is so great,
the sorrow so intense,
the confusion so overwhelming
that we think we cannot possibly endure.

Yet, in those very moments
God's love can be so real,
His presence so unmistakable,
and His peace so calming.

He offers to wrap us
in arms of peace,
fill us with an everlasting joy,
and shower us with unconditional love.

God is simply waiting
to enter our lives,
to forgive us our failures,
and to give us hope.

Our difficulties may remain,
but we no longer have to carry them alone.
God will not leave.
He will not fail.
God is ever present God.

The LORD himself goes before you and will be with you; he will never leave you nor forsake you. Do not be afraid; do not be discouraged.

Deuteronomy 31:8 NIV

- Diana C. Derringer

43

Five Ways to Bless Your Home During Advent

Christmas time's a comin'
Christmas time's a comin'
Christmas time's a comin'
I know I'm going home.

The bluegrass Christmas song reminds us of the coming of Christmas. Parents plan for its coming. Churches celebrate the season. Children longingly anticipate December 25. My son Dawson grimaced last year, and said, "It seems like it takes forever for Christmas to get here."

Expectation and anticipation mark believers in God today, and historically. Abraham and Sarah waited for God to fulfill His promise to give them a son. David longed for a temple in Jerusalem where they could worship Jehovah. The prophet Isaiah exhorted the people to expect God to comfort and deliver them. The magi followed a star, expecting the celestial sign to take them to the King of the Jews.

Since the ascension of Jesus Christ, believers have awaited His return. The Greek word *parousia* means "coming" or "arrival." The New Testament uses the word seventeen times to describe the Second Coming of Christ. Translated from the Greek *parousia*, the Latin word *adventus,* means "arrival or coming." For Christians, advent specifically signifies the four weeks leading up to Christmas Day.

W. T. Ellis said, "It is Christmas in the heart that puts Christmas in the air." The advent season can be a great time for families to celebrate Jesus Christ afresh. Parents are wise to create opportunities for children to focus on Jesus amidst all of the holiday rush.

Five ways we might help our families celebrate advent.

1. Family Devotions. Hold family devotions, also called family worship or the family altar, at least once a week during December. Pick four characters from the Christmas account in the scriptures. Each week, read the Bible passages about that person and discuss their story. What did Joseph learn about trusting God? What did it cost Mary to obey the Lord? What did Simeon learn about waiting on God? Why did God appear to shepherds and not important people in society?

   See what lessons you can glean about being a modern-day disciple of Jesus Christ from these Christmas characters. Find a Christmas song or carol that goes along with the character you focus on weekly. Introduce the song to your family at a meal. Sing the song together that week during family worship.

2. A Jesse Tree. This ancient tradition, based on Isaiah 11:1, helps children creatively learn the Christmas story and related scriptures. Some people find a live or artificial small tree. Others cut a tree out of construction paper and tape it to a wall. Pick out twenty-four Bible stories and create small ornaments that correspond with each story. Artistic people may want to create elaborate ornaments. For simple people like me, construction paper, scissors, and crayons suffice. Each day of advent, read and discuss the related scripture and Bible account and then hang or tape one ornament on the tree. My daughter Anna-Frances told me, "Daddy, I like doing the Jesse Tree because I get to make something with my hands."

3. A Prayer Garland. Cut out twenty-four green and red construction paper strips. On each strip write the name of one family member, friend, or ministry. Then staple the strips into one long garland. Hang the garland in your apartment or house as a decoration. Some years our garland goes directly on our Christmas tree. Every day in December, allow one family member to take off one of the paper strips. Pray for the name on that strip of paper as a family during the day. You may want to even call and encourage the person.

4. The Advent Box. Several years ago I purchased a wooden box, painted with beautiful nutcrackers all over the front. The box has twenty-four small doors that open to a hiding place. The first week of advent I place small toys, candies, and inexpensive gifts behind each door. I divide the twenty-four days of December by my three children and assign each child eight days of the month. Each morning of December, one child opens the Nutcracker box and finds the surprise. My children enjoy the fun and daily anticipate the surprise.

Charles Dickens said, "It is good to be children sometimes, and never better than at Christmas, when its mighty Founder was a child Himself." The advent box tradition creates a spirit of anticipation in the home and is loved by our children.

5. Christmas Cards. Cheri Fuller shares this idea in her book *When Families Pray.* As Christmas cards arrive during December, put them in a basket at a noticeable place in your house. Once a day, perhaps over a meal, pull out one card and pray for that person or family together. One year we kept the Christmas card basket out all year and prayed regularly for other families. You may want to jot the person a note signed by your family that says, "We prayed for you today."

Frank McKibben said, "This is Christmas: not the tinsel, not the giving and receiving, not even the carols, but the humble heart that receives anew the wondrous gift, the Christ."

Practicing these simple activities can help families open our hearts afresh to the living Lord Jesus. We won't just be waiting for Christmas. We'll be celebrating Christmas

~ Dr. Rhett H. Wilson, Sr.

44

Where Is Baby Jesus?

Where Is Baby Jesus?

The nativity display in our small town park featured some of the main characters in the depiction of the birth of Jesus Christ. Mary was present; Joseph stood faithfully by; the angels were ready to sing; and the three magi were on the scene. But where was Baby Jesus? The space in front of Mary and Joseph was completely bare; not even a manger was placed before them.

In the past there had been problems with vandals stealing the doll that had been placed in the manger. Perhaps those in charge of decorating our park had grown tired of replacing the doll and opted to present the nativity scene minus the central figure. The park was beautifully illuminated with a rainbow of colors. Much labor and time had gone into preparing the park for the Christmas season, but without the Baby Jesus, the true meaning of Christmas was missing.

Many people decorate their homes for this special time of the year. Their trees may range in size, from small ones placed on tabletops to large ones touching high ceilings. The decorations may be homemade: popcorn and cranberries strung on a long thread and wrapped around the branches. Others may be elaborate and cover the trees with gold and silver ornaments and a bounty of twinkling lights.

Nativity scenes are brought from storage and placed on table-tops and under the decorated trees. Each piece is carefully arranged and usually centered around the manger with the Christ child in it.

Perhaps we could see that missing baby Jesus from the manger as a reminder that, yes, he was born as a baby, and that should be celebrated, but he's not there anymore. He lived, grew, died, and rose from the grave. If we believe and accept that, then Jesus is in our hearts here on earth, and we will be with him eternally in heaven.

As we carefully decorate our trees and our homes, and as we rush about buying gifts to give to our loved ones, do we pause to prepare our hearts and our lives to welcome this Gift who was given to us over 2,000 years ago?

Do we stop to ponder the words of John 3:16? The words that are so familiar that we quote them without stopping to think what they actually mean. Wasn't Jesus Christ the most precious, most sacrificial Gift that God could give to the world?

~ Norma C. Mezoe

After Christmas

Songs of Christmas still echo
with warm gladness in my mind.
Bright Advent candles linger
as Christ's beacon to be kind.

When I observe pain-worn faces
and many who suffer loss,
I recall how the Lord Jesus,
poured compassion from a cross.

If I could create a symbol
of all Christ has truly borne,
I'd stand those Advent candles
in a triumphant crown of thorns.

~ Charlotte Adelsperger

A Christmas Prayer

Lord, please just let us know by Christmas if she is alive.

This was my daily prayer. It had been six months since our daughter had disappeared. At times, the pain of not knowing where she had gone and if she was alive became unbearable. Daily I immersed myself in the Psalms. I had told our three other grown children that we needed to not let her absence destroy our joy and love of living. We had long since given her up to God.

It seemed like yesterday that she had been a vibrant healthy teenager who loved clothes, her friends and all the other normal activities of her teen years. She attended a Christian High School.

The past two years had been very traumatic for our family. My brother died suddenly at age fifty-three of a heart attack. Then six months after his death his wife was murdered. Our favorite uncle, who our daughter was close to, died. All of these painful events took place within six months. They had taken an enormous toll on our family.

I appeared to be handling the horrific events well. But that was not true. I only stuffed the pain and grief deep within me. I fell into a depression. I had a difficult time *being there* for my family.

Through all these events this darling girl of ours changed. Her preferred clothing color became black. One day she came home from a friend's house and she had cut her long blond hair and dyed it black. Although I was shocked, I thought, *Well she is 18 and attending City College. She is studying art. I guess she is just trying to look artsy.*

She also had a new boyfriend of whom I was very leery. He was rail thin, extremely pale and had a cold demeanor about him. When I commented on that, our daughter told us it was because he had a heart condition. Her entire personality began to change. I tried every method of communicating with her. I asked her if she used drugs. She became upset and gave many excuses for her changed appearance and behavior.

One day I had to drive forty-five miles to direct a live performance of *The Fanny Crosby Story* at a convention center. Thousands of people were expected. I needed to get cash from our bank but when I went to the ATM I found that my bank card was missing. I went into the bank to see if there had been any recent activity on my account. Hundreds of dollars had been taken out. Suddenly, the horror of the mystery of what was going on in my daughter's life came to me.

My head began to spin. My heart pounded so hard I could barely breathe. I jumped into the car and drove the two blocks home and rushed into the house. "Jill," I called, "Where are you?" I found her upstairs in her room. "I know you have my debit card and you have been robbing us. You have taken hundreds of dollars from our account. I want you to give me that card this minute." Her expression was flat and cold as she handed me the card.

"Why, why have you done this? What has happened to you?" Her hazel eyes appeared almost black and her mouth clenched tight with defiance when she answered, "Heroin."

At last I had the hideous answer to what had stolen our daughter's life.

"Jill," I said "If you don't stop using this drug you will be dead."

She said, "I'd rather be dead than stop."

"Honey," I cried. "I love you. Nothing you can ever do will make me stop loving you. If you want to get well, we will help you. We will get you the help to stop using."

My heart broke as she responded again with a look of total defiance and hatred.

"Jill, you were planning to move to your own apartment in two weeks and have already packed most of your things. Get the rest of them together now. You have to leave. You are not a safe person. Please call a friend to come and get you."

I felt the mighty power of God holding me in His arms as I watched her move her belongings to our front porch and walk down our walkway and out of our lives.

With calm beyond my understanding I called a fellow director and told him what had happened. I asked him if he could come with me as I sat in the director's box to call the show. I knew I couldn't do it with a clear mind. He agreed and drove me there. Another television director friend came along.

These men love the Lord and prayed with me during the drive.

I didn't call my husband who was in New York on business. How could I tell him over the phone that our baby girl was a heroin addict? I would wait until he returned.

During the performance I felt God's presence in the director's booth as I called the show. I stayed the night with my director friend and his wife. Sleep was impossible.

With eyes swollen from tears that would not stop I cried out to God, "Oh Lord, my baby, my Jill. How can this be? How could I have failed to see? I love her with all my heart. What did I do wrong? Our other kids are fine. Please forgive me for failing her. Help her, save her."

At 3 A.M. I fell to the floor and said, "Lord, she is yours. You take her. I know You love her more that I do. I give her to You." After my surrender, sleep finally came.

My husband returned from New York and I had to tell him what had happened to our Jill. Then he had his night of sorrow and grief.

A few weeks later we heard from Jill. She seemed desperate. She said she wanted help and agreed to go into a rehab hospital. We were overjoyed. At last she could leave drugs. She could start a new life. Our girl had come back to us.

When she left the hospital we helped her find an apartment. She got a job. We kept in contact daily.

One day the phone rang and a voice asked if I was Mrs. Mead. "Yes," I said, "how may I help you?"

"I'm Jill's boss at her work. She was supposed to work today but when I came in, the store wasn't open and the cash register has been cleaned out. I cannot reach Jill by phone."

My labored breath came in spurts. "Thank you for letting me know."

I rushed to her apartment. Her landlady let me in. It was in shambles. On the wall was a large drawing. As I viewed it I felt that my breath was being sucked from me. At one end of the drawing was a figure dressed in white with a halo over his head. He appeared to me to represent Jesus. In the middle of the drawing was a lake, burning with fire. At the other end of the lake was a figure that looked evil, and was dressed in black. A caption coming from his mouth read, "You can never go back."

Our hopes were dashed again. Six months went by. I kept asking God to please let us know by Christmas if she was dead or alive.

With God's help we lived as normally as possible. The Christmas season came. Everywhere were colorful decorations, parties and celebrations. As we decorated our tree, my heart warmed as I hung each ornament our children had made. Tears fell as I held the ones Jill had made. While I cooked our traditional Christmas Eve food I thought of Jill and the dishes she loved. The smells of our traditional Christmas Eve fare wafted through the house as we waited for the kids and the grandkids to arrive.

Just as we were going to sit down for our supper the phone rang. A very faint voice said, "Mommy? This is me, Jill. I'm only a half hour away. I'm clean and sober. Can I come home?"

Can she come home? "Yes, yes, yes!" I cried. My husband drove to get her. When they got home we celebrated the most joyous Christmas we had ever experienced.

Later, when our other children left I held Jill in my arms and she told me of her decision. "I was sitting on the floor of an abandoned building all strung out on drugs and said to myself. I don't have to live like this. I have a family who loves me. I can go home."

As she continued to live a healthy life, a few friends asked why we had taken her back after all she had done. They felt she didn't deserve it. I agreed, "No, she didn't deserve it but we took her back because we love her. She is our child. Our love for her does not have conditions."

Later as I pondered their questions I was reminded that when I came to Christ many years ago with my broken life, I asked him to forgive all my sins. Did I deserve it? No, but He did it because He loved me and I became His child. He continues to forgive me each time I sin because He loves me even though I don't deserve it. He does this because I'm His child.

My prayers were answered that Christmas when our precious child came home to us. Overwhelming joy filled my heart that night as I thanked our Heavenly Father who gave us the gift of his only Son. Why did He do it? He did it because He loves us.

- Suzanne Liggitt

47

Where's the Gravy?
A Southern Tradition
at Christmas

Southern gals know how to make gravy. It's one of those unspoken prerequisites for coming of age in the South and getting married to a Southern guy.

Types of gravy come in the boatfuls — you've heard of the "gravy boat." Red-eye gravy. Chocolate gravy. Turkey gravy. Tomato gravy. But I'm referring to breakfast gravy, usually sausage-flavored, poured over piping-hot Southern biscuits.

For twenty years my husband, Mike, served as a youth pastor. He now holds the lead pastor position at our church. Mike grew up on Southern gravy, as did I. Many of our pastor friends often discuss whether there is food in heaven and if it's Southern favorites like pinto beans and cornbread…and gravy!

As a good Southern gal and pastor's wife, I learned how to make gravy early in our marriage. Over the years, I prepared Southern gravy countless times — Saturday morning family time and special occasions.

Still to this day, I often cook a Southern breakfast for dinner and I'm always serving gravy on holidays. Like some restaurants that serve breakfast all day and every day, Karen's Kitchen is always open for gravy.

So of course a huge Southern breakfast on Christmas morning is a family tradition. My husband, my adult son and daughter, my son-in-law, and other relatives come to our home for this spread.

What I call "gravy trauma" occurred while making traditional gravy on one such occasion. Anyone who has made gravy can attest to the occasional splatter of grease popping out on a hand or arm.

While I worked with a spatula for the right consistency, a large amount of hot floured grease landed on the top side of my left hand.

An immediate, intense, severe burning sensation hit the nerve endings on my skin. Discolored in a disgusting brownish-green tint, it formed a big blister. Karen's Kitchen would not be serving gravy that day. Instead, a nasty burn served up a relentless dose of pain.

My husband worried I might never make gravy again, likening it to a real emergency situation. I'm happy to report I have made gravy since the "gravy trauma." But I knew I would not come out of the ordeal physically unscathed. I would have some semblance of a scar. No hiding the scar. No camouflaging. Clothing would not cover it. Cosmetics might help minimally.

The healing process took about six weeks. Today, I bear a scar on the top of my hand.

Healing from an injury — even after the completed process — often leaves a mark behind, a record that *something happened there.*

It reminds me of a friend who bears a scar on his hands. Two scarred hands. Nails placed them there. Nails pounded into a wooden cross. Jesus' scars on his hands, his feet, and his sword-pierced side, wounds from floggings, and stripes on his back. Why? Because *something happened there.*

Christ suffered excruciating pain through beatings and crucifixion, dying on a cross so we could have eternal life. He was wounded for our transgressions, he was bruised for our iniquities; the chastisement of our peace was upon him; and with his stripes we are healed. (Isaiah 53:5 KJV)

Especially at Christmastime, when celebrating the birth of Christ, and I see my scar, I don't feel my pain, but I think of his scars. He suffered his willingly, because God so loved the world — me — that he gave his Son Jesus, so that whoever believes in Him shall not perish, but have everlasting life.

~ *Karen Friday*

48

Growing the Gift of Prayer

For years, our large extended family met on Christmas Eve to celebrate Jesus's birth. The mood was merry and festive as three generations gathered around the tree to exchange gifts. But as my nieces and nephews grew up, I found it harder to find gifts that suited them. Their toys were no longer inexpensive matchbox cars or plastic tea sets. At a loss for ideas, I prayed, "Lord, I need help. What gifts could make a lasting impact?"

Then a thought came to me: What about the gift of prayer? That certainly fit our budget.

But prayer would cost time. I couldn't give everyone this gift because I wouldn't have time to keep my promise. I decided to start with my oldest niece, a recent college graduate who was teaching vocal music to junior high students. Since I was a former teacher of teenagers, I certainly knew she needed prayer.

I began mulling over how to package my gift. While shopping, I found a small ceramic planter shaped like a school desk. A sign on the desk read, "Closed for Christmas Vacation." How perfect! I bought the planter along with a prayer plant (*Maranta leucoreura*) to place inside it. Since the variegated leaves of this plant fold up each evening, like hands placed together in prayer, it would remind my niece of my prayers.

That year at our Christmas Eve family gathering, I gave Ann the planter and plant, along with a coupon that read: "I commit to pray for you once a week for one year." Ann loved the gift and offered to send me specific prayer requests.

To help me keep my commitment, I set aside a specific weekly time to pray for her. Since Ann was a music teacher, I prayed for her during my children's weekly piano lessons. That year of teaching could have been difficult for her since she replaced a popular teacher. But as it turned out, Ann's students loved her, and her classes earned music awards. Although Ann worried her class enrollments would be small the following year, she felt overwhelmed by the number of students who requested her classes.

146

When my year of prayer for Ann ended, I was free to give someone else this special gift. But I continued to pray for Ann as God brought her to mind. Years later, I asked Ann — by then a mother with two preteen daughters — what she thought of my gift of prayer that Christmas. She said, "That's the best gift anyone could have given me. You could give it to me *every* year."

Later, when my older sister (Ann's mother) was diagnosed with cancer, I gave her a prayer plant and a get well "heal-ium" balloon. I added a note saying, "The balloon is to lift up your spirits, and the plant is to remind you that I'm lifting you up to God." God certainly answered those prayers for healing. Decades later, my sister is a vibrant, active senior citizen. What a joy to see! I'm glad God chose to heal her. Over the years, I've reaped many blessings from my sister as she models how to grandparent, age gracefully, and serve others (including me during a season of illness).

Prayer is a priceless gift that fits any budget. And unlike other gifts, one size fits all. The gift of prayer comes wrapped in love, tied with heartstrings, and yields eternal benefits. And no one will exchange your gift.

Would you like to bless someone with the gift of prayer? Here are some suggestions for giving this lasting gift.

1. Ask God who needs the gift of prayer.
2. Give the gift only to those you can faithfully pray for.
3. Set aside a specific time when you will pray (weekly, or as often as you have time).
4. Ask for prayer requests or a favorite scripture passage to use in prayer.
5. Consider sharing this gift not only for Christmas, but also for birthdays, graduations, and during illnesses.
6. Give the gift with or without a prayer plant. (A plant can be a tangible reminder of your prayers.)
7. Expect blessings as you watch God answer and grow this gift of prayer!

~ Lydia E. Harris

49

Christmas...Why Bother?

Cast of Characters:

LTM – Little Trouble Maker: played by Toni's problem fabricator

SA – Spirit Angel: played by Toni's yearning soul

Opening Scene:

It's several weeks before Christmas and Toni has been waiting to see if her Christmas will, yet again, be spent alone. She doesn't want to be a "humbug" about Christmas but when you're all alone there just doesn't seem to be much reason to celebrate. The scene is anywhere around her home, that isn't decorated. When you live all alone, and there is no joyous coming together of family and friends, why bother?

Quiet Internal Conversation:

LTM: "Christmas is just like any other day. When you spend it alone, separated from family, it's not anything special.

SA: "Wait a minute! I think it's special."

LTM: "Really? Well, exactly what makes it special? Do you plan to cook a scrumptious turkey dinner just for you? NO.

Do you have a ton of presents under the tree to open? NO. You don't even have a tree.

Are you going to sit around and have a lot of fun conversations and laughter with your dog? NO. So, what makes it special?"

SA: "Well, it all depends on why you celebrate Christmas."

LTM: "For the gifts and the food, what else is there?"

SA: "For Jesus."

LTM: "For who?"

SA: "For Jesus. It's his birthday were celebrating."

LTM: "So, are you going to bake him a cake? How about the ice cream? You can't have a birthday cake without ice cream. And candles; are you going to light candles?"

SA: "No, no, and no. But during the season I'm going to sing him lots of birthday songs."

LTM: "You are going to sing Happy Birthday to him? Don't you need to pay someone a fee if you want to sing that song?"

SA: "Technically, the fee is only required if you're singing it publicly or for money. There you go trying to get me off track with your silliness. No, I'm going to sing about him, about his birth and all the wonderful things that happened to announce that he had come into the world. You know that he is the most famous person that was ever born. He's God's Son — his only son. He was born for a very special reason. He was born to tell us about his father. He spent three years, from age thirty to age thirty-three picking out men and women to help him spread that word around the world. He taught them about the importance of worshipping and glorifying his Father, the Creator."

LTM: "Jesus was just a prophet, a man."

SA: "Jesus was human, that's true. But Jesus was also divine like God, his Father. Have you never read about Jesus? About all the things he did while He was on earth? He healed the sick, and made the blind see, he raised the dead and taught us how to love one another. When his job was finished he died, a horrible death on the cross, taking all the sin of the earth with him so that we could be united with his Father and live with them forever. We celebrate his birth at Christmas and his death at Easter, on Resurrection Sunday."

LTM: "So, let me get this straight. We celebrate his birthday, okay — check. But, we celebrate his death? Who does that? And Resurrection Sunday? Are you telling me he came back to life?"

SA: "Exactly. Just like all his believers will do, someday."

LTM: "This is just too much for my little brain. So, let me recap. You are going to be alone on Christmas Day, with a few presents, no big meal, no games, no enticing conversations and you still think it's a special day?"

SA: "Well, for a little while I didn't, but after talking with you about it I certainly think it's a very special day that will always be worth celebrating, no matter what the circumstances. How about you? Do you want to join me? I think I'll set up my nativity scene, decorate my tree, and I might even purchase a small turkey to cook. It will make the house smell good. And, I'm going to play some Christmas songs on my CD player and sing along."

(SA starts humming "Silent Night.")

LTM: "I still say, Why bother?"

SA: (With a big smile on her face.) "Why bother with Christmas? Because it's not about me, or about you, it's about him. Happy Birthday, Jesus. Let's celebrate!"

~ Toni Armstrong Sample

50

Sharing the Gospel from My Exploding Closet

I pressed down on the plastic shoebox lid while trying to cram a stuffed bear's arm back into the box. The lid snapped just as the arm cleared the side. I slipped a couple of heavy duty rubber bands on to keep the top from popping off again.

There! My two boxes for Operation Christmas Child were done.

I thought back to the early days when our family first started packing shoeboxes for the Samaritan's Purse ministry to distribute around the world. My son would pack a boy box making sure to include a ball and a toy car, and my daughter would lean towards all things sparkly and Barbie.

This year was different, with my son now a college student and my daughter, a year behind him, currently overwhelmed with school obligations.

I didn't even mention the boxes to her. I just did them myself. I wondered if I would continue to do them after she left for college.

Soon after I finished my boxes, my friend Dolly visited and I met her for coffee. I first met her at a writer's conference, and we didn't see each other often because we lived quite a distance from each other. I happened to mention the shoeboxes, and learned that all by herself, she had packed dozens of boxes that year.

I put my coffee cup down, amazed. "How do you do it?" I knew from experience it had always cost around twenty-five dollars for us to pack just one shoebox. Financially, it seemed impossible for us to pack dozens. Yet, I knew Dolly lived on a budget, too.

"I shop all year," she said. "I look for markdown items after Christmas, Valentine's Day, Easter, and other holidays. "

She made it sound so easy. *Could I could do that, too?* I wondered. I'm in the stores a good bit for other reasons.

A few days later after I had prayed about it, I thought I would at least try for a larger number. For the next year, I set what I thought was a lofty goal — twelve boxes.

If I was going to pack that many boxes, I had to be especially thrifty. I followed Dolly's example, shopping after holidays, when retailers marked down their seasonal merchandise to clear it. I searched for items reduced to seventy-five percent off — socks, coloring books, and toys. I bought many for as little as a quarter. When school supplies were reduced, I picked up crayons, markers, notebooks, and pencils. I purchased balls reduced from summer stock.

One thing I didn't scrimp on, and that's a toothbrush that wouldn't make gums bleed. Children in the third world may not have brushed regularly, so I thought it important to buy a good soft toothbrush. Also, I tried to manage a light up toy or flashlight and include extra batteries. If a child lived without electricity, I knew these things would be a wonder. I once heard someone who traveled with Operation Christmas Child say to never send a boy box without a toy car, because no matter where they are in the world, it's the first thing boys look for when they open their boxes.

After a year of piling things into my guest bedroom closet, in November, I opened the door and an avalanche of stickers, pencils, hairbrushes, coloring books and other items spilled out. With a little tweaking, I managed to put together twelve boxes for Operation Christmas Child. Six boys and six girls.

I couldn't believe it. As I loaded the boxes into my car, I stood back and imagined the children's faces when they opened them. Joy!

The next year, I aimed for sixteen boxes, the next twenty, and the next twenty-four. My guest bedroom closet almost exploded.

Then a couple of years ago after a series of unfortunate financial reversals, I came up short in September when I reviewed what I needed to finish. What would I do? I hated to reduce the number of boxes. I thought about my sister, Tammy. She had not participated in the ministry up to that point. I called her and explained the situation. She jumped at the chance to be involved.

For the last couple of years, my sister and I get together and spend an entire day packing twenty-four, twenty-five, and sometimes twenty-six boxes. We fill our boxes to within a hairsbreadth of not closing.

Here is what especially motivates me: I heard a testimony recently from a missionary in Eastern Europe who spoke about how important the shoebox ministry was in bringing children to his church. Because of Operation Christmas Child, he had opportunity to share the Good News with so many who had never heard it before.

When I look back at how I wondered if I would continue packing two boxes, I am amazed that by God's grace, Tammy and I now pull together over ten times that many.

Would you consider joining us in putting smiles on children's faces and sharing the Gospel with them?

You can download "How to Pack a Shoebox" and labels for the boxes from Samaritan's Purse at https://www.samaritanspurse.org/operation-christmas-child/pack-a-shoe-box/. Pay special attention to the items that shouldn't be included. A toll-free number for drop off locations is provided or you can mail your shoeboxes to Operation Christmas Child headquarters in North Carolina.

Happy packing! I hope your guest bedroom closet is bigger than mine.

- Beverly Varnado

51

Putting Christmas Away

I've put Christmas away
for another year,
the trimmings and wrappings
and times of good cheer.

The tree, once adorned,
stands shamefully bare
of the tinsel and bulbs
once hung there with care.

The gifts under the tree
are all stored away;
now little is left
of that wonderful day.

Yet, I'm reminded
that's only one small part.
The important thing is
to keep Christmas
tucked away in my heart.

- Norma C. Mezoe

Divine Moments Series Guidelines

If you have been entertained by, inspired by, or simply enjoyed the stories in this book, we'd love to hear about it. Perhaps you'd like to share your own story(ies) in one of our other planned Divine Moments books.

Send your personal articles!

Take a look at previous Moments books that Grace Publishing has released to see what we accept. The article length is anywhere from about 500-2000 words or so. I've even included poems and some pieces written by children. So the guidelines aren't strict. The main point is the context of the article. I like them sent as an attachment to an email, Times New Roman, 12-point type.

These may be original or previously published if rights have been returned to you. We retain rights after acceptance until the book is published, then rights automatically return to you. Include on the article: your name, mailing address and phone number for your one free copy, and email address. Send to me at: yvonnelehman3@gmail.com

Already published are: *Divine Moments, Christmas Moments, Spoken Moments, Precious Precocious Moments, More Christmas Moments, Stupid Moments, Additional Christmas Moments, Why? Titanic Moments,* and *Loving Moments.*

We're accepting submissions for:

Coola-nary Moments — culinary mishaps or unusual cooking experiences, recipes. I have one about making mud pies when a child. (This book is almost filled.)

Romantic Moments — falling in love, puppy love, marriage, dating, second time around, weddings, flowers, mother-of-bride, bridesmaids, anything to do with personal love or planning a wedding, etc.

Questionable Moments — author's response to questions asked by God/ Jesus in the Bible, or implied, such as "Where are you?" "Where are you going?" "Do you love me?" "Do you believe?" "Where is your faith?" "What do you want?" Or when you questioned God.

Personal Titanic Moments — Highs and Lows of Life — grandeur and/or disaster

Broken Moments — lives, hearts, marriages, promises, bones, mirrors, etc.

Another Christmas one for 2018.

No payments. Authors receive one free copy, discount on orders, and all royalties go to Samaritan's Purse, an organization that helps victims of war, poverty, natural disasters, disease, and famine with the purpose of sharing God's love through his son, Jesus Christ. www.samaritanspurse.org

The articles are written by both multi-published, and beginning or non-published writers. This is a way of giving to the world, all year long.

www.yvonnelehman.com

About the Authors

Charlotte Adelsperger is an author and speaker from Overland Park, Kansas where she lives with her husband Bob. She has taught writers' workshops in six states. Charlotte has written four books and material for more than 100 publications and compilations. Her poetry has appeared in numerous magazines and gift books. Charlotte writes for both adults and children. Most recent is her children's picture book, *Amazing Miracles of Jesus*, illustrated by Nancy Mungers.

Betty Mason Arthurs is a grandmother and great-grandmother who enjoys life in the southwest. She writers devotions, stories about her years as a nurse and humorous articles about aging.

Sheryl M. Baker is an award winning author who enjoys sharing hope and encouragement through God's Word. Her devotions have appeared in *Power for Today, Light from the Word, the Secret Place* and *ChristianDevotions.us*. She is a contributing author to *Spoken Moments, More Christmas Moments*, and *Loving Moments*. Sheryl also maintains her blog *Spun by the Potter: Life Lessons Uniquely Created by God*. To see more of Sheryl's writing visit spunbythepotter.com or sherylmbaker.wordpress.com. You can connect with Sheryl on Facebook at https://www.facebook.com/sheryl.m.baker. Sheryl lives in Northwest Indiana with her husband, Ben, and enjoys spending time with her children and grandchildren.

AimeeAnn Blythe is a freelance writer, published author, and is currently working on ideas for books in three different genres. Her two furry children are by her "creative" side every step of the way. info@aimeeannblythe.com.

Tez Brooks is an award-winning author and speaker who writes on family issues with some of his work appearing in *The Upper Room, Clubhouse, Focus on the Family*, CBN.com and Cru.org. His book, *The Single Dad Detour* was winner for the 2016 Royal Palm Literary Awards. His screenplay *Jangled*, won 2016 Best Short Film in Florida at CENFLO. Tez is a member of Word Weavers International, American Christian Writers Assoc., and Florida Writers Assoc. Tez loves time-travel movies and the color orange. He and his wife serve as full-time missionaries with Cru. They have four children. You can read more from Tez at EverySingleDad.com.

Rebecca Carpenter, an award-winning author, writes at her lake retreat near Orlando. After retiring from teaching elementary school, she and her husband traveled the world for missions and pleasure. Experiences with her granddaughters, traveling, and nature inspire her writings which have appeared in *Adventures in Odyssey, Clubhouse* magazine, *Posh Parenting, Christmas Moments, Celebrating Christmas with…Memories, Poetry and Good Food.* Her book, *Ambushed by Glory in My Grief,* consists of devotions during her grief journey after losing both her husband and parents within a short time. You may visit her at http://rebeccacarpenter.blogspot.com.

Lauren Craft believes our Heavenly Father gives each of His children a purpose, and fulfilling His plan is one of the greatest joys we can experience before reaching our eternal home. Besides writing, God has blessed Lauren with opportunities to aid in Bible translation and share the gospel on four continents. You can connect with her at www.laurencraftauthor.com.

Pat Jeanne Davis writes from her home in Philadelphia, Pennsylvania. She is wife to John and Mom to John and Joshua. She enjoys flower gardening, genealogy research and travel. Her work appeared in *Guideposts, The Lookout, Bible Advocate, Faith & Family, GRIT, Splickety, Sasee, Ruby for Women, Woman Alive* and *Chicken Soup for the Soul* books. She writes historical inspirational novels and is a member of American Christian Fiction Writers. Pat loves to hear from her readers. Visit her at www.patjeannedavis.com.

Lola Di Giulio De Maci is a retired teacher whose stories have appeared in numerous editions of *Chicken Soup for the Soul, Los Angeles Times, Sasee* and *Reminisce* magazines, as well as children's publications. Lola has a Master of Arts in education and English. She writes overlooking the San Bernardino Mountains. You may contact her at LDeMaci@aol.com.

Diana C. Derringer is an award winning writer and author of *Beyond Bethlehem and Calvary: 12 Dramas for Christmas, Easter, and More!* She enjoys traveling with her husband and serving as a friendship family to international university students. Her blog at www.dianaderringer.com helps people with a non-English background understand the meaning of unusual English expressions and offers a brief respite for anyone who enjoys word play. https://dianaderringer.com/

Julie Dibble, MA is a Christian speaker and author who has a passion for truth. With a late-in-life transformation, Julie is forever grateful for Jesus. She and her husband Jason live in Central PA with their sons, Braedon and Jackson. Julie writes at her blog www.juliedibblewrites.wordpress.com and has two published articles in *Purpose* Magazine. Julie will speak to both secular and faith-based groups: MOPS and other women's groups, retreats and conferences. You may connect with her: http://www.juliedibble.com/; https://www.Twitter.com/@julie_dibble; https://www.Instagram.com/@jayjule03; https://www.Facebook.com/jdibble4Him/. Lyrics of "Silent Night" taken from www.christmas-carol-words.com

Kristin Tobin Dossett lives in Kentucky with her husband and three young boys. She is a nurse practitioner and sonographer at Alpha Pregnancy Care Center. She enjoys blogging at www.lovemercywalkhumbly.com. Her writings can also be found in the books *Additional Christmas Moments* and *Loving Moments*.

Terri Elders received her first byline in 1946 on a piece about how bats saved her family's home from fire, published on the children's page of the *Portland Oregonian*. At nine years old, she hadn't known that her title, "Bats in Our Belfry," would lead readers to suspect her family's sanity. Her stories have appeared in over 100 anthologies. She can be contacted at telders@hotmail.com.

Peggy Ellis has been a freelance editor for 40 years, and an author for considerably less. Over the past 25 years, she has published regularly in such magazines as *Good Old Days*, *Reminisce*, *Rock and Gem*, *Aquarium*, *True Story*, *Splickety*, *Woman's World*, and *Righter Monthly Review*, now *Righter Quarterly Review*, the latter in print and ezine. She has compiled and edited three anthologies for her writers' group: *Challenges on the Home Front World War II*, *Lest the Colors Fade*, and *A Beautiful Life and Other Stories*. Each contains her short fiction, memoirs, and research.

Gayle Fraser has published a junior high girls' curriculum, *Dove*, on self-identity and what Scripture says about being a young lady in Christ. She has written curriculum, and developed a weekly prayer group for Christian grandmothers titled *Grandma's Faithfulness Pray Warrior*. She has also written curriculum, *Shush, I'm a Secret Sister*, for women who would like to come along with a pre-teen, promoting Christ-like characteristics and lifestyles through being a secret sister. The program is a year-long process with all details developed. *Oreo Floppy Tail*, *Mama and Her Five Munkies*, and *My Home Sweet Home* are three children's books she has written, illustrated and one has been self-published. *Love Stories from Grandma's Heart* was written for her grandchildren. She is currently writing a devotional, *Abba's Whispers*. In her busy life, she and her husband have smuggled Bibles into China, participated in the Billy Graham Crusade in Moscow, Russia; toured Israel, and Gayle took her granddaughter to Hungary with her church's youth group.

Karen Friday is a pastor's wife and women's ministry leader. She's an award-winning writer and avid speaker who loves words and God's Word. Karen earned a communications degree and has experience in a broad spectrum of business services where she is frequently referred to as Girl Friday. A blogger, Karen "Girl" Friday engages a community every week. *Hope Is Among Us* is an award-winning blog that expresses scriptural truths as life happens. Karen has published a number of articles and devotions in both print and online media and writes as a regular contributor for the national site, *Inspire a Fire*. She is currently working on her first book project about God's goodness and mercy. Karen and her husband Mike reside in Johnson City and have two grown children and a grandson. The entire family is fond of the expression, "TGIF: Thank God It's Friday." They owe Monday an apology.

Tommy Scott Gilmore, III is a gifted speaker, teacher, motivational leader, and Executive Director of Changing Lives Ministry (http://www.changinglivesministry.info/). Tommy is a graduate of Taylor University and Gordon Conwell Theological Seminary having a B.S. and a Master's in Education. He is published in *Decision Magazine, The Christian Athlete, The National Network of Youth Ministries, Single Minded, WNC Parent,* and numerous articles in *Youth Specialties Encyclopedia for Youth Workers.* He wrote a Bible study in conjunction with music for Steven Curtis Chapman's "For The Sake of the Call." He is author of two training manuals, *A Comprehensive Pro Life Resource for Ministers, Politicians, Pro Life Workers,* and *Teachers & Changing Lives Training Manual for Youth Workers* which has been used by numerous youth pastors in over 29 states and missionaries in 7 countries. He has contributed stories to *Christmas Moments, More Christmas Moments, Merry Christmas Moments, Divine Moments, Spoken Moments* and *Stupid Moments.* Other than being introduced to his best friend ever, "Jesus Christ," after his atheist father attempted to kill Tommy on 5 different occasions, the greatest joy of his life was to fall in love with 7 of the most beautiful women in the world. Beginning with the prettiest, they are his wife Sandra, his 3 daughters Lindsey, Brittany and Meghan, followed by his granddaughters Sarah and Victoria and concluding with the most charming 4-legged creature (with a tail that never stops waging) – Miss Annie of Augusta and her brothers, Kirby and Mr. Finnegan (Finn).

Gigi Graham is the eldest daughter of Ruth and Billy Graham. She is the mother of seven grown children, grandmother to twenty grandchildren — so far — and seven greats. Gigi's experience as the daughter of a well-known evangelist, raising seven children, living in both the Middle East and Europe, has given her many resources for her writing and speaking ministry. She serves as Ambassador of the Billy Graham Training Center at The Cove in Asheville, North Carolina. Gigi is an award-winning author of several books including *Weather of the Heart, Currents of the Heart* and *A Quest for Serenity*. She divides her time between central Florida and the mountains of North Carolina and can be contacted through Ambassador Agency in Nashville, Tennessee.

Lydia E. Harris has been married to her college sweetheart, Milt, for 50 years. They have two married children and five grandchildren ranging from age seven to eighteen. Lydia earned a Master of Arts degree in home economics. She has written numerous articles, book reviews, devotionals, and stories. *Pockets* and Focus on the Family's *Clubhouse* magazines for children publish her recipes, which she develops and tests with her grandchildren. She writes the column, "A Cup of Tea with Lydia," and is called Grandma Tea by her grandchildren. Lydia has contributed to thirty books and is author of the book, *Preparing My Heart for Grandparenting: For Grandparents at Any Stage of the Journey*.

Helen L. Hoover and her husband are retired and live in Northwest Arkansas. Sewing, reading, knitting, traveling, and helping her husband with home repair occupy her time. *The Secret Place, The Quiet Hour, The Lutheran Digest, Light and Life Communications, Chicken Soup for the Soul,* and *Victory in Grace* have published her devotionals and personal articles. Visits with their two living children, grandchildren and great-grandchildren are treasured.

Cynthia Howerter is a speaker and award-winning author whose passion is historical fiction. A member of the Daughters of the American Revolution (DAR), she is thrilled to live in history-rich Virginia with her husband. Cynthia and La-Tan Roland Murphy co-authored *God's Provision in Tough Times*, a non-fiction anthology. Visit Cynthia on Facebook, Twitter, www.ColonialQuills.blogspot.com, and www.cynthiahowerter.com.

Alice Klies has written since she could hold a pencil. She is currently president of Northern Arizona Word Weavers, a chapter of an international writers group. Through their encouragement Alice began to submit her work for publication. She has nonfiction and fiction stories published in 16 anthologies. She is a seven-time contributor to *Chicken Soup for The Soul* books and has articles in *Angels On Earth, AARP* and *Wordsmith Journal*. She has been featured in the *Women of Distinction* magazine. Besides her involvement in Word Weavers, she serves on boards for the PWG (Professional Women's Group) and Y.E.S. the ARC in her community. She is a deaconess and Stephens Minister in her church. Alice is a retired teacher who resides with her husband and two Golden Retrievers in beautiful Cottonwood, Arizona. She prays her stories cause a reader to smile, laugh or cry, and most of all turn their eyes upward to God who loves them.

Samantha Landy is a member of AWSA, a Guideposts Advisory Cabinet Member and a two time Angel Award winner from Excellence in Media. Samantha has worked in media for over 30 years. She hosted/produced a Christian TV show *Something Beautiful* in the San Francisco area, and appeared in many Christian TV shows including *700 Club* and TBN. Her articles appear in *Women's Aglow, Guideposts* (the *Plus* Magazine) and numerous other publications. For years she wrote a weekly newspaper column, "The Way...As I See It," and a singles column for *Significant Living* magazine. She founded Christian Celebrity Luncheons in 1986 which has hosted a dynamic list of Christian celebrities, bringing the good news of the love of Jesus into the country club world of southern California. Northwood University recently named her Distinguished Woman of the Year at a Black Tie Gala in Phoenix.

For twelve years she has hosted an international radio program, *Psalms of Hope*, which is heard on secular and Christian stations in the U.S., as well as broadcasting out of Jerusalem going into the Middle East and beyond. *Psalms of Hope* is also on Short Wave radio in the 10/40 window. *Psalms of Hope and Courage*, a 365 devotional, makes twelve books Samantha has authored. She has contributed to four compilations and ghost-written two books. She and her husband, Randy, will host a tour to Israel along with Pat Boone in May, 2018. You may reach her at: www.SamanthaLandy.com and Facebook.com/theSamanthaLandy.

Yvonne Lehman is a best-selling author of 58 novels and compiler of 10 non-fiction books. She founded and directed the Blue Ridge Mountains Christian

Writers Conference for 25 years and now directs the Blue Ridge "Autumn in the Mountains" Novelist Retreat held annually in October. She has joined Lighthouse Publishing of the Carolinas as Acquisitions and Managing Editor of Candlelight Romance and Guiding Light Women's Fiction. She earned a Master's Degree in English from Western Carolina University and has taught English and Creative Writing on the college level. Her recent novel releases are a novella *Have Dress Will Marry (Heart of a Cowboy* collection, *Better Latte than Never* (cozy mystery), and 8 Romances (4 set in South Carolina, 4 set in North Carolina). Her non-fiction Divine Moments series is published by Grace Publishing. For release in 2017 are *Merry Christmas Moments* and *The Gift (Secret Admirer* collection). Her 50th novel is *Hearts that Survive – A Novel of the Titanic*, which she signs periodically at the Titanic Museum in Pigeon Forge Tennessee. She blogs at www.christiansread.com and Novel Rocket. www.yvonnelehman.com - yvonnelehman3@gmail.com

Suzanne Liggitt is a member of Northern Arizona Word Weavers. She grew up in Pasadena, California and lives in Cottonwood, Arizona with her husband, Jack. With their combined families, she and Jack have 8 children, 19 grandchildren and 6 great-grandchildren. She has been an inspirational speaker for over 40 years for retreats, schools and churches. She worked on stage as a singer, actress and director as well as Production Director in Christian Motion Picture and Associate Director of the *Something More* television show.

Diana Leagh Matthews is a vocalist, speaker, writer, and genealogist. During the day, she is a certified Activities Director for a nursing facility. She is a Christian Communicators graduate. She has been published in several anthologies, including several Moments books. She currently resides in South Carolina. Visit her at www.DianaLeaghMatthews.com; and www. alookthrutime.com.

Beverly Hill McKinney has published over 300 inspirational articles in such publications as *Good Old Days, Breakthrough Intercessor, Just Between Us, Woman Alive, P31* and *Plus Magazine.* She has devotions in *Cup of Comfort Devotional Daily Reflections of God's Love and Grace, Open Windows, God Still Meets Needs and God Still Leads and Guides.* Her stories have been featured in anthologies such as *Christmas Miracles, Men of Honor, Guidepost's Extraordinary Answers to Prayer, Christian Miracles, Precious Precocious Moments* and *Additional Christmas Moments.* She has also self-published two books, *Through the Parsonage Window* and *Whispers from God: Poems* ⟨ *Inspiration*. She graduated from the Jerry B. Jenkins Christian Writer's Guild and lives in Oregon.

Mary E. McQueen has served for many years as an ordained minister. She has lived in many states and completed studies in Europe. She and her husband Ken (also ordained) live and serve churches in Lincoln, Nebraska. They have five grown children. Mary has served as a police chaplain and is a facilitator in the Anti Violence Project inside prison walls. She and her husband are childbirth and gentle parenting instructors. She has coached and helped deliver a large number of healthy babies as part of her ministry. For more information, visit her blog at pastormcqueen.com.

Andrea Merrell is an associate editor with Christian Devotions Ministries and Lighthouse Publishing of the Carolinas (LPC Books). She is also a professional freelance editor and was a finalist for the 2016 Editor of the Year Award at BRMCWC. She teaches workshops at writers' conferences and has been published in numerous anthologies and online venues. Andrea is a graduate of Christian Communicators and a finalist in the 2015 USA Best Book Awards. She is the author of *Murder of a Manuscript, Praying for the Prodigal*, and *Marriage: Make It or Break It*. For more information, visit www.AndreaMerrell.com or www.TheWriteEditing.com.

Norma C. Mezoe has been a published writer for 30 years. Her writing has appeared in books, devotionals, take-home papers and magazines. She lives in a tiny town in Indiana where she is active in her church as clerk, teacher and bulletin maker.

Vicki H. Moss is Contributing Editor for *Southern Writers Magazine*, a previous newspaper columnist, author of *How To Write For Kids' Magazines* and *Writing with Voice*. With over 500 articles published internationally, she's written for several magazines and was selected to be a presenter of her fiction and creative nonfiction short stories for three consecutive conferences at the Southern Women Writers Conference held at Rome, Georgia's Berry College. Vicki is a speaker and on faculty for writers conferences. For more information about Vicki visit livingwaterfiction.com.

Karen Lynn Nolan is a writer, actress, musician, artist, Kentucky mountain storyteller, and mom. Her love of mystery and suspense means she usually includes a dead body in anything she writes. Her first Appalachian novel releases in late 2018. Karen is an award-winning writer and has pieces included in several anthologies. Karen's mission as she writes about her journey through natural disasters, chronic illness, depression, homelessness, several near-death experiences, late-life divorce, and financial ruin is to show others how to find joy during adversity.

Dr. Jayce O'Neal is the pastor of RED Church in Virginia Beach. RED Church is a growing church community focused on helping others discover REDemption through Jesus. Dr. Jayce is also the author of the best-selling *One-Minute Devotions for Boys*, *No Girls Allowed: Devotions for Boys*, *Crazy Circus World* and *100 Answers to 100 Questions Every Graduate Should Know*. He is an Instructor at Regent University and is an avid sports fan who enjoys cheering for his favorite teams while eating pizza with a fork. Dr. Jayce has a Doctorate, two Masters Degrees, a Bachelor of Science, and a small trophy for perfect attendance in Sunday school from when he was nine. He currently resides with his fantabulous wife and three children in the Virginia Beach area. For more information visit: redchurch.tv.

Sally Wilson Pereira is a Billy Graham Team kid, former BGEA staff member, friend, pastor's wife and widow, Mama and Grammy. Through these unique roles God has given her the opportunity to serve Him and minister to others. She's travelled the world and owns stories of God's grace in times of both happiness and suffering. Sally lives in Black Mountain, North Carolina. Her greatest joys are her daughters, Emily Meyer and Mary Pereira, and her four grandchildren.

Deborah M. Presnell is a published author, national speaker, workshop presenter, and a partner with the Polished Conference Ministries L.L.C. She facilitates an online Bible study on Facebook, teaches Bible study in her church, and blogs at *Shining Together!* Debbie has written *Shine! Radiating the Love of God*, a Bible study designed exclusively for young women ages 13-18. She is a monthly contributor to *Refined* Magazine and the Polished Conference blog. She would love to speak at your next women's event, teen event, or at the college where she brings an inspirational message to teachers in training titled "A Christian Perspective for an Inspirational Classroom." Debbie is married and has three adult children. She travels from Asheville, North Carolina. Visit her website at www.debbiepresnell.com, email her at: debpres@yahoo.com, or visit her page on Facebook: https://www.facebook.com/ShineEveryDayNC.

Colleen L. Reece describes herself as an ordinary person with an extraordinary God. Raised in a home without electricity or running water but filled with love for God and family, Colleen learned to read by kerosene lamplight and dreamed of someday writing a book. God has multiplied her "someday" book into *150 Books You Can Trust*, with six million copies sold.

Robert B. Robeson has been published 900 times in 325 publications in 130 countries. This includes *Reader's Digest, Positive Living, Writer's Digest, Frontier Airline Magazine,* and *Newsday,* among others. Robeson has also been featured in 55 anthologies. He's been a newspaper managing editor and columnist, has a BA in English from the University of Maryland-College Park and has completed extensive undergraduate and graduate work in journalism at the University of Nebraska-Lincoln and is also a professional (life) member of the National Writers Association. He lives in Lincoln, Nebraska with Phyllis, his wife of 48 years.

Toni Armstrong Sample retired early to Greenwood, South Carolina at the end of a successful career as a Human Resource Executive, with the final fifteen years as the Owner/President of an HR Consulting and Training firm that she founded. Toni has written for professional journals, recreational magazines, devotionals, newspapers, and inspirational story publications. Her first inspirational romance novel, *The Glass Divider,* was released in 2014 followed by *Transparent Web of Dreams, Distortion,* and *A Still Small Voice.* Her first non-fiction book, *I'll Never Be the Same,* written to bring hope and healing to those going through traumatic experiences, was released in February, 2017. Released in August, 2017 was *A Buck Three Eighty: A Baby Boomers Stories About Growing Up in the North.* Watch for future books in 2018, all available on Amazon.com and at Barnes and Noble. Toni is a Christian retreat leader, conference speaker, Christian education and women's Bible study facilitator. She is a commission artist concentrating on painting biblical scenes and characters.

Annmarie B. Tait resides in Conshohocken, Pennsylvania with her husband, Joe Beck. In addition to writing stories about her large Irish Catholic family and the memories they made, she enjoys singing and recording Irish and American folk songs with her husband. Among her other passions are cooking, sewing and crocheting. Annmarie has over 50 stories published in various anthologies including *Chicken Soup for the Soul* and the *Patchwork Path* series. You may contact her at irishbloom@aol.com.

Beverly Varnado's work has been a finalist for the prestigious Kairos Prize in Screenwriting, a Gideon screenplay finalist, and a semifinalist in Christian Writer's Guild Operation First Novel. She has a screenplay under option as well as two novels in print, *Give My Love to the Chestnut Trees* and *Home to Currahee*. She writes regularly for *The Upper Room* magazine and her work has been featured on World Radio. She has over seven hundred posts on her blog, *One Ringing Bell: peals of words on faith, living, writing and art*. Her work was included in another anthology this year, *Short and Sweet*. She has a new non-fiction book releasing in 2018, *Faith in the Fashion District, How One Woman's Life on Seventh Avenue Launched a Lifetime in Ministry*. She is also a working artist and recently exhibited at a state university. gallery.www.BeverlyVarnado.com, OneRingingBell.blogspot.com.

Judith Vander Wege, Christian freelance writer/composer/Bible study leader, has been published in many Christian periodicals and a newspaper. Formerly an RN, she obtained a B/A in music ministry as a senior citizen. Judith has been a member of the Lutheran, Foursquare, and C&MA denominations previously to marrying her current husband, Paul, in 2006. They attend First Reformed Church in Orange City, Iowa. Her passion is to help hurting people get into an intimate relationship with God, to experience his love and healing.

Dr. Rhett H. Wilson, Sr. is an award-winning freelance writer who blogs at www.rhettwilson.blogspot.com. Rhett teaches Bible as an Adjunct Professor of Christianity at Anderson University. He and his family live in upstate South Carolina. The Wilsons like playing board games and exploring waterfalls, and they look forward to March Madness every year. For fun, Rhett reads legal thrillers and listens to Broadway, country, and symphony music.

CPSIA information can be obtained
at www.ICGtesting.com
Printed in the USA
FFOW04n1534171117
43515423-42244FF